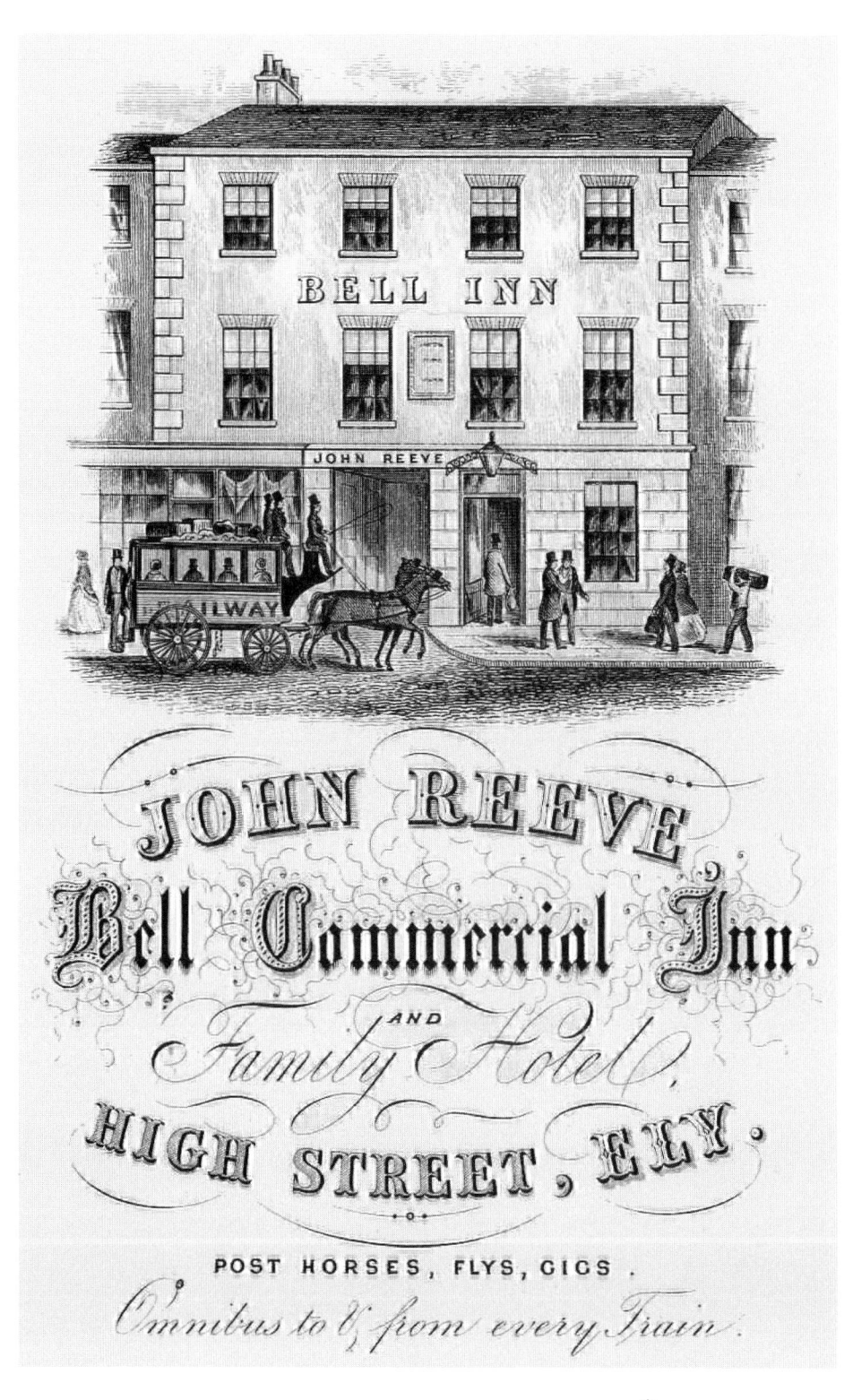

A Bell Hotel billhead dating from the middle of the 19th Century.

ELY INNS

A HISTORY OF ELY INNS AND BEER HOUSES.

by
PATRICK ASHTON

Incorporating original material
by
Reg Holmes and Pamela Blakeman

Published by The Ely Society.
2007

CONTENTS

Frontispiece 2
Forword 5
Preface 5
Introduction 6

The Anchor 9
The Angel 10
The Baron of Beef 12
The Bell Inn 13
The Black Bull 15
The Black Swan 17
The British Sportsman 18
The Chequers 18
The Club Inn 20
The Coach and Horses 22
The Coopers' Arms 23
The Cromwell Arms 24
The Crown and Anchor 25
The Crown 26
The Crown Inn 27
The Cutter 29
The Dog and Gun 32
The Dolphin 34
The Duke of Wellington 36
The Duke of York 37
The Eagle and Lamb 38
The Elephant and Castle 39
The First and Last 39
The Five Bells 40
The Fountain 40
The George and Dragon 41
The Glaziers' Arms 43
The Globe 44
The Green Man 45
The Hammer and Trowel 46
The Hereward 47
The High Flyer 47
The Jolly Farmers 49
The King Charles in the Oak . . 50
The King William IV 51
The King's Arms 52
The Lamb 54

The Maid's Head 58
The Malt and Hops 58
The Marquis of Granby 59
The Minster 60
The New Inn 61
The Oddfellows Arms 62
The Peacock 62
The Plough and Fleece 64
The Prince Albert 65
The Queen's Head 66
The Railway Inn 67
The Railway Tavern 68
The Red Lion 69
The Red, White and Blue 72
The Rifleman 73
The Rising Sun 74
The Rose and Crown 75
The Round of Beef 76
The Royal Oak 77
The Royal Standard 78
The Ship 79
The Star 81
The Sun 82
The Three Blackbirds 83
The Three Crowns 84
The Three Cups 86
The Tinker of Ely 86
The Town House 88
The West End 89
The Wheatsheaf 90
The Wheel 91
The White Hart 92
The White Lion 96
The White Swann (Mkt St) 98
The White Swan (Waterside) 98
The Windmill 99
The Woolpack 100

FOREWORD

I have known Mr. Holmes for more than twenty years, and have never ceased to admire his industry, persistence and ingenuity in the pursuit and publication of information about Ely. This is his final work, which Miss Pamela Blakeman has edited and prepared for publication and which displays all the qualities I have mentioned. But there was much more to Mr Holmes than this: no one who met him or asked for help from him, can have failed to appreciate his unfailing kindness, his generosity of spirit and his readiness to share his knowledge with others. These are wholly admirable traits in any scholar, but much more admirable in one whose knowledge had been acquired so laboriously, and in the face of so many difficulties, as his. Such acts of generosity are, regrettably, unusual, and when they are done in such a cheerful and affectionate spirit, as his were, rare indeed. We shall sorely miss his friendship and his help.

I am very glad to pay this small tribute to him, and to have been associated with his work

Dorothy Owen. 1984.

PREFACE

The above Forword by the late Dr. Dorothy Owen has been reprinted as a continued tribute to the late Reg Holmes. To this must be added an appreciation of the industry, persistence and expertise of Patrick Ashton who has contributed a great deal to this new revised edition and has added much to our knowledge. Reg Holmes would have been delighted, as indeed I am, to know that an able and younger man has taken on his role. The Ely Society Publications Sub-Committee would like to congratulate Patrick on his first impressive venture into local history publishing.

Pamela Blakeman 2007.

INTRODUCTION

The study of inns, alehouses and beer houses can give a real insight into the social and economic history of any community revealing the growth and development of that town or village. Ely is a particularly rewarding subject as it is large enough to support a considerable number of licensed houses yet not too large to make it difficult to trace the fortunes of the various premises.

Throughout history there is documentary evidence of the existence of inns and brewing in the City. This evidence is to be found in many and diverse documents. In the records of the Bishop's Manor for the year 1250 it reveals that the Bishop's tenants had to provide three men at Whitsun to hoe in the Episcopal orchard and that these three men were not to go to the inn before evening.

In 1575 the Churchwardens of St. Mary's Parish recorded in their accounts that year that "...*the stoke is converted into forty coomes of maulte.......wiche maulte do Remayn in Robert Silvertope's to the use of the parysh*". Sivertop's maltings were situated near the Malt and Hops public house in Church Lane. There was at one time a footpath leading from these premises through the Churchyard to St. Mary's Green.

The naming of inns in this country became common in the 12th century and as the majority of the population could neither read nor write, the pub sign was the favoured way to advertise their existence. In 1393 King Richard II passed an act requiring "*Whosoever shall brew ale in the town with intention of selling it must hang out a sign, otherwise he shall forfeit his ale*", so that official ale tasters could identify them.

The 18th Century saw a significant increase in the number of public houses, mainly due to the introduction of gin. Gin was brought to England by the Dutch after the "Glorious Revolution" of 1688, also government policy of the time had allowed unlicensed gin production, whilst placing heavy taxes on all imported spirits. As gin-shops became prolific all over England, the local brewers fought back by increasing the number of alehouses. The Gin Act of 1736 imposed higher duty on retailers which led to widespread opposition. The prohibitive duty was gradually reduced and finally abolished in 1742. But by 1740 gin production had increased to six times that of beer and due to its cheapness it became popular with the poor leading to what was known as the "Gin Craze". Ale continued to be popular, as it was considered safer to drink than water, but the drunkenness and unruliness created by gin was seen to lead to the downfall of the working classes. The subsequent Gin Act of 1751 was more successful however as it required distillers to sell only to licensed retailers and as such brought the gin-shops under the jurisdiction of the local magistrates.

In 1753 another act was passed which required local magistrates to only grant licences if the applicant had a Certificate of 'Good Character' signed by a parish 'notable'. It also stated that a full Register of Victuallers be made and to be kept by the Clerk of the Peace at Quarter Sessions. These became the first recordings of licensed businesses.

By 1821 concerns for the conduct and activities of the working classes saw landlords being fined or losing their licenses if they were to "*suffer Gaming with Cards, Draughts, Dice, Bagatelle, or any other sedentary Game in their houses, or any Part of their premises;..... nor to permit or suffer Bull, Bear or Badger-baiting, Cock-fighting, or other such sports or Amusements;..... not to keep open the same at late hours of the Night or at early Hours in the Morning*'.

An act that was passed in 1830, "The Beer House Act", had a major impact on the history of the public house. This allowed anyone who paid the poor rates to obtain, on payment of 2 guineas to the authorities, a licence to open their house and sell beer or cider for six days a week not including Sunday, with extended opening hours of 4.00am to 10.00 pm. Often it was just a front room of a house or shop, and thus, what became the Victorian back street pub was born. The passing of this act was to try and reduce the consumption of gin and resultant lawlessness that had ensued, however, within eight years the number of beer houses had nearly reached that of inns and alehouses. The increase in demand for hops and barley for brewing saw a boom for many farmers, some of whom themselves started brewing beer.

Unsurprisingly the introduction of the beer house did little to reduce the effects of drunkenness and lawlessness until the "1869 Wine and Beer Act" was passed which brought in stricter controls by requiring each premises to obtain a valuable license from magistrates. These stricter controls included regulation of opening hours, gaming, drunkenness and unlawful conduct, which would result in the landlord losing his license. These licenses would be granted, renewed or transferred annually at special court sessions, later to be known as Petty Sessions. Also for the first time ever, detailed records would be kept by the Court Clerk, thus providing the first proper records for tracing an inn or pub's history.

To try and reduce the number of inns and pubs that had opened during the 19th century a new act was passed in 1904 which required detailed plans to be submitted for each licensed premises to the courts and allowed for compensation to be paid for the withdrawal or transfer of a license. Usually it was the older, more expensive to repair houses, which were closed allowing the newer ones to prosper.

Initially most inns brewed their own beer, but by the mid 19th century, with the change in licensing laws, independent commercial brewers were supplying beer houses and some inns. As business grew, the brewers bought the premises and as such, the tied pub was born. Ely's independent brewers belonged to the Cutlack, Hall, Harlock and Legge families. In 1907 Cutlack merged with Harlock and in 1910 they acquired Legge's business, they in turn merged with Hall in 1930 to form the well-known Hall, Cutlack & Harlock, brewers of Ely Ales. In 1950 they were merged with Huntingdon Breweries to form East Anglian Breweries. Then in 1960 Steward & Patteson took over the business followed by Watney Mann in 1967, who closed the brewery in 1969 thus ending the history of commercial brewing in Ely. One other brewery in Ely was the Eagle brewery in Cambridge Road that was owned by Richard Porter. In 1889 he sold it to Morgans of Norwich who closed it in 1902.

The number of public houses around the Waterside area during the 18th century reflects the amount of business and industry that was being carried out in that part of Ely, the Quayside being a hive of activity then. By the mid 19th century with the arrival of the railway the number of pubs around the southern end of Broad Street and Station Road area saw a marked increase to cater for the trade that the railway bought to the city. In 1851 there were in excess of 68 drinking establishments open in the City. By the turn of the 20th century it had reduced to 61. Pubs around this time were often used for meeting places, inquests and auctions. Many also ran a slate/share-out club, which on regular payments being made into the club gave members the benefit of sick pay, Christmas share out and death expenses

The effects of changes in licensing laws and the loss of riverside industries saw many pubs struggle to survive, and together with the ensuing takeover of small family run breweries by the larger businesses, rationalisation plans saw many pubs fall by the wayside and in 1960 just 24 public houses remained open. Today the City of Ely has just 10 licensed public houses open, two of which have opened in the last 12 years. The main areas of concentration for public houses of the mid 1800s like Newnham, Newtown (Cambridge Road), Waterside, Broad Street and Station Road which were served by several pubs now see one, if any, surviving in those communities.

Whilst most inns and pubs have been researched there are a few that have not been mentioned as either their name or the location is unknown. Reference to a "*beer house*" or a licensee's conviction with no premises mentioned, is often the only indication of ones existence, so these have not been included. On many occasions there is more than one person named in the license records for a particular pub, where this is the case only the first name has been used.

ACKNOWLEDGEMENTS

I would like to thank the many people who have kindly assisted in a variety of ways and those who have allowed the use of their material in this publication including Chris Jakes and the Staff of The Cambridgeshire Collection, The Staff of The County Records Office, Cambridge, Clare Turner of The Cambridge Magistrate's Courts, Pam Blakeman and other members of the Ely Society Publications Sub-Committee and Lesley Oakey. Also those who have provided pictures: that on page78 Ely Museum, those on page 52, and the Round of Beef in the 1930s on page 76 Michael Rouse. Other pictures were provided by Pam Blakeman or the author.

Also I would like to acknowledge the use of information from *The Roll of Honour* website for information about Reg Seekings of the Rifleman's Arms.

The author has done his best to trace ownership of all pictures and would like to apologise if any have not been acknowleged.

Published by The Ely Society 2007.
Copyright © P Ashton and The Ely Society.
Printed by Ely Print Centre.
ISBN 0 903616 23 8

ANCHOR

The former Anchor public house in 2007.

The Anchor was situated on Waterside at what is now number 2, Waterside and number 58, Fore Hill, and carried an "old license" which meant it could serve beers, wines and liquors.

When Nash & Co of Royston sold off their brewery business in 1852 the auction particulars for Lot 33 described the property as *"A Brick and Tile DOUBLE HOUSE, occupied by JOSEPH CHAMBERS and H.MAUNGIER, with TWO SHOPS in Front, large GARDEN and YARD behind, Range of Stabling and Lodges; together with a Slaughter-house, and Entrance into Back Lane"*. Lindsells of Chatteris bought the Anchor for 355 guineas and supplied the pub up to its closure in 1909.

The Returns of Licensed Houses in 1906 shows the Anchor as having 3 bedrooms for family use, 3 bedrooms for lodgers and stabling for 1 horse.

The Anchor closed its doors for the last time under the 1904 compensation scheme. The property is now a private residence.

1790 - 1790 Thomas Vail	1859 - 1863 No records
1791 - 1800 Edward Bromfield	1864 - 1866 William Gotobed
1801 - 1812 John Spenceley	1867 - 1868 Presumed shut
1813 - 1815 Robert Eaves	1869 - 1869 John Ablet
1816 - 1831 James Nethercoat	1870 - 1872 Ann Ablet
1832 - 1850 John Gotobed	1873 - 1876 Alexander Kerr
1851 - 1851 Mary Ann Gotobed	1877 - 1891 William Benton
1851 - 1858 Joseph Chambers	1892 - 1909 Charles Henry Beezley

ANGEL

Mr Stedman with his wife and daughter.
C. 1930, taken by Tom Bolton.

The Angel in 2007

The Angel was situated at number 24, Station Road, previously known as Bridge Road, and is now used as a business premises.

The history of the Angel certainly goes back to the 17th century, as in a survey made by Thomas Bullis for the Manor of Ely Porta in 1679 there are references to a *"tenement abutting upon stone bridge toward the North and upon the road leading to High Bridge toward the East"*. This evidently refers to the Angel as Christopher Emerson is shown as the occupant and he was admitted to the premises on the surrender of John Garland in 1672. In 1708 Mrs Elizabeth Stallon, whose mother had been an Emerson, took over. In 1751 there is a reference to a Bill of carpenter's work, which includes an item of 4 Shillings *"to 2 Days work of a man"* and was *"Don at the Angel Near Stonebridge"* (this stone bridge referred to, is shown on Speed's map of 1610). Accounts dating from the same period refer to a quit rent of 3s.6d. paid by Jonathan Page *"for the estate late Mrs Stallons"* and received on 29th October 1749. Mr Page's right to the messuage under Mrs Stallon's will was challenged by James Burroughs of Cambridge as in a letter *"you must defend and defend rightly or you will loose your estate"*, however Jonathan Page was admitted to the property in 1755. In 1797 Thomas Page took ownership as a copyhold admission contained a list of a number properties including a messuage *"formally Christopher Emerson's near Stonebrdge and now the sign of the Angel"*. Thomas also provided sureties together with licensee John Berry of £1.17.6.

During this period meetings, inquests and other events took place at the inn. On 11th April 1763 a *"meeting of the Turnpike Trust for the road from Ely to Soham ordered that a Toll Gate be forethwith erected between the Angel Corner and Caudwell Fen Drove"*.

From 1850 to 1853 the landlord, John Reeve, also held the license for the refreshment rooms at the newly built Eastern Counties Railway Station.

An advert appeared in the Cambridge Chronicle on 18th June 1853 " *TO BE LET-THE ANGEL INN, ELY, with possession 6th July next, situate in the immediate proximity to the railway and having an extensive and increasing Business attached. The Inn has been enlarged and adapted to the requirements of the trade of the important railway junction which it accommodates, and there being excellent stabling for 60 Horses, a steady livery, Trade is added to the Business*".

The Angel had its own brew house to supply its beers until it became one of Henry Hall's premises. In 1906 the Angel was shown to have 4 bedrooms available to lodgers and 3 for the licensee's use, with stabling for 4 horses, a reflection of the times, with the decline in horse drawn traffic compared to 53 years earlier. The Hall family owned the Angel up to 1930 when they merged with Cutlack & Harlock, it then passed through Steward & Patteson, and Watney Mann ending up as a Pubmaster house. The Angel held a full alehouse license until closure in October 1995.

1790 - 1797 John Berry	1892 - 1892 Albert Pitter
1798 - 1805 William Rickwood	1892 - 1901 James Speed
1806 - 1812 William Merrill	1902 - 1904 John Dobbs
1813 - 1815 Bailey Stimson	1905 - 1908 Albert James Smith
1816 - 1831 Robert Eaves	1909 - 1910 Fred A Rains
1832 - 1846 William Fuller	1911 - 1925 Charles George Griffin
1847 - 1853 John Reeve	1926 - 1947 Clarry Vince Stedman
1854 - 1857 Mary Reeve	1948 - 1954 William Francis Claxton
1858 - 1861 John Moore	1954 - 1962 John Wm Jenkins
1862 - 1864 Francis Cropley	1962 - 1974 Henry Badger
1865 - 1886 John Tibbles	1975 - 1993 Alex Allen
1887 - 1887 George Squire Demiss	1994 - 1994 Allen Ramsey
1888 - 1888 William Brown	1994 - 1994 Allen Medlock
1889 - 1891 James William Legge	1995 - 1995 Malcolm Daily Berry

The Angel Tap

As with many Inns, the Angel had a "Tap bar" for the use of non-hotel guests, the entrance of which was nearest the road and is now bricked up.

During redecorating in 1863 this lettering was revealed across the face of the building :-

MOORE'S COMMERCIAL & FAMILY HOTEL

It was no doubt painted between 1858 and 1861 when John Moore was licensee.

The City of Ely Fire Brigade engines were housed in the stables on the corner of Gas Lane (Croyles Lane) and Angel Drove in 1892. The Turncock was F M Maynard, the Landlord of the Angel Tap. He was responsible for turning on the water supply that was drawn from Cawdle Fen Drain. The water would have been pumped into a tank drawn by horses to the site of the fire and discharged onto the fire from the manually operated pump.

BARON OF BEEF

The Baron of Beef was situated at 13 Fore Hill, mid way on the north side where Griffin antiques is now. It started out as an eating-house, which would indicate the origin of its name, and became licensed premises during the mid 19th century when it was licensed as a beer house.

The Baron of Beef during Joseph Nightingale's time and an advert from a local trade directory.

An agreement dated 4th January 1866 Stated "*William Cutlack of Littleport, Common Brewer, and Joseph Nightingale of Ely, Shoemaker. To rent All that Messuage or Tenement situate on Fore Hill in Ely, called The Baron of Beef, at rent of £12 per annum. And shall and will during his tenancy take, have and purchase from William Cutlack all the table beer, porter and all which he Joseph Nightingale shall use or sell*".

The "Baron" had 5 bedrooms, 2 of which were available to rent for lodgers or travellers. On the right hand side as you entered was the Taproom and bar, all beer was drawn straight from the barrel. During Joseph Nightingale's time the room to the left of the entrance was used as a shop, to sell and repair musical instruments. At the rear was a large dining room, which was particularly popular on market days.

From 1913, after Joseph Nightingale left, the "Baron" was owned and supplied by Bailey & Tebbutt's brewery of Cambridge

Around 1939 - 1945 the Baron of Beef was a favourite with the women's land army and unsurprisingly was very popular with the servicemen, so was often full to capacity on a Saturday night.

The license was surrendered in 1958 when it closed. The property was later demolished and rebuilt as Evans Tailors and menswear.

1858 - 1865 Henry Bailey
1866 - 1912 Joseph Nightingale
1913 - 1915 Edward George Parker
1916 - 1919 Arthur Charles Smith
1920 - 1920 Wilfred Clarke
1920 - 1927 Thomas Edwards

1928 - 1933 William Collen
1933 - 1937 Frank Blaker
1937 - 1939 Charles Henry Oxbrow
1940 - 1951 Smith Searle
1951 - 1958 Sidney Lorell Rains

BELL INN

The Bell Inn circa 1910 and as it is in 2007.

At 19, High Street was situated the Bell Hotel, nearly opposite the Goldsmith's Tower, that housed the bell, which was rung, for funerals and weddings when services were held in Holy Trinity Parish Church (the Lady Chapel). This is where the name is likely to have come from.

The earliest reference to the Bell is in Holy Trinity Churchwarden's Accounts, where William Brabie and Robert Morgan presented their accounts in 1588 *"Elyie Trinitie, The Accompts of Wm. Brabie and Robert Morgan taken before Wm Styward Esquire, Robert Cropley, Gent, Wm. Cranforde, Clement Hinde with other inhabitants of the said parish xxth Janurie Ao Dni 1588"*. They spent eighteen pence and on 23rd January sixteen pence at The Bell.

In 1608 and 1610 the commissioners, presumably of the Bedford Levels, paid Mistress Martyn at the Bell varying sums. In 1612 Thomas Styward handed over to the Court Leet and Baron of the Manor of Ely Barton a garden lying between *"Coxe Ponde"* and the tenement called The Bell and half an acre lying in the Ely fields upon Hangman's Hill. The gallows from which Hangman's Hill takes its name lay on the right of the present road leading from Ely to Witchford.

The Thomas Parsons' Charity Governors met in 1667 at the Bell, being the house of John Squire at *"3 of the clocke in the afternoon"*. And elected Benjamin Laney, Lord Bishop of Ely to be Governor of Parsons' Charity. The Bell continued to be mentioned as a meeting place for the Governors, Bailiffs and Conservators of the Bedford Level, who held a committee there in 1676, and in the same year the Parsons' Charity Governors expended at Mr Squire's three shillings. In the following January a further sum of two shillings and eight pence was expended at

Mr Squires' house when "*wee waited upon the Deane about he letting of Tom's Hole*" in the fen near Adelaide.

On the occasion of the birthday of His Majesty King George the Third the following was printed in Cambridge Chronicle on 8th June 1799 "*Amidst the general display of loyalty on His Majesty's birthday on Tuesday last the association of Ely ought not to pass un-noticed. This truly respectable corps consisting of 100 effective men assembled in honour of the day under arms early in the morning and had a grand field day on which they performed their difficult evolutions with a correctness that reflects the greatest credit on the assiduity and attention of their officers and the zeal and patriotism of the respective members. On leaving the field they partook of an elegant dinner at the Bell Inn, and spent the afternoon with that heartfelt enthusiasm inspired only by a sincere love for their Sovereign, their Laws, their Religion and their Liberties*".

In 1824 the stage coach named the Union which ran from King's Lynn called at the Bell three mornings a week on its way through Cambridge, Barkway, and Ware to London and on alternate days it travelled in the opposite direction, passing through Littleport to Downham Market. The Telegraph travelled between Cambridge and Upwell via Ely, calling at the Bell on three days a week, at eight in the morning, and on the return journey at seven in the evening. Other carriers were Brands & Son's, whose wagons called at the Bell at 2 o'clock on the way to London on Mondays and Thursdays, and Thomas Browning who was taking the carriers' cart to Littleport every evening.

Robert Wade, the landlord in 1842, was petitioning the Governor, Baliffs and Conservators of the Bedford Level asking them to consider his inn as a place for their meetings. He stated that "*the inn has been lately rebuilt on an extensive scale and furnished and fitted up at a very considerable Expense and is now well calculated to afford every requisite Accommodation to visitors, especially to those who are engaged in public Business*".

By 1850 the inn had its own omnibus, which awaited the arrival and attended the departure of all trains at the Great Eastern Railway station. The landlord in 1852, was advertising in the Cathedral handbook "*BELL INN, and, Commercial House, High Street Ely, William Briggs, Excellent Beds, Wines and Spirits, of Superior Quality, Good Stabling, An omnibus to and from every train, Post Horses, Flys Gigs etc*"

The Bell occupied quite a large plot, stretching back from the High Street towards Butchers Row, which included good stabling. In 1906 it was shown to accommodate 15 horses and 15 vehicles.

Mary Reeve fell foul of the law when on 10 December 1875 she was "*fined £10 plus costs for allowing gaming for money with cards and also charged with refusing entry to PC Colman*".

By the end of the 19th Century the Bell Hotel housed a Railway Receiving Office, from which the parcels cart left for the station at frequent intervals during the day.

The hotel was often used to hold auctions, including local properties "*On Thursday, 17th November 1921 at 4p.m. precisely*" some important properties in Ely came under the hammer of George Comins, Ely Auctioneer and Land Agent and included "*A Modern Residence. Erected in 1915, with Garden situate on the*

Lynn Road'. Then in the occupation of Mrs J. Cutlack this is now number 11 Lynn Road. Number 5 too, formerly the residence of Mr H.S. Wallis (father of Ken Wallis of autogyro fame) now part of the office accommodation of East Cambs District Council, was offered for sale.

The Bell held a full alehouse license until its surrender on 21st May 1960. During its history, Henry Hall, A&B Hall through to Steward & Patteson, have owned it. In its last year, the Bell was under the same management as the Lamb and served as a bedroom annexe to the more important inn until its closure.

1608 - 1610 Mistress Martyn	1880 - 1885 Edward Fredrick Baines
1667 - 1677 John Squire	1886 - 1888 Kate Taplin Baines
1790 - 1792 Joseph Garner	1888 - 1892 Charlotte Harriet Davis
1793 - 1793 No return	1893 - 1923 John Charles Laxton
1794 - 1795 Jonathan Spenceley	1924 - 1927 Charles James Matthew Hobson
1796 - 1799 Jonas Taylor	
1800 - 1800 No return	1928 - 1930 Francis Charles Tomkins
1801 - 1811 John Hawkins	1931 - 1933 Emily Dodman
1811 - 1822 John Spenceley	1933 - 1934 Edwin Martin
1823 - 1824 Ann Spenceley	1934 - 1935 Walter Charles Bartram
1825 - 1840 Thomas Spenceley	1936 - 1942 William Ingham
1841 - 1847 Robert Walker	1943 - 1943 Elsie Amy Price
1848 - 1850 Caroline Walker	1944 - 1950 William Ingham
1851 - 1852 William Briggs	1950 - 1955 Millie Kenderdine
1853 - 1853 John Reeve	1955 - 1956 Air Vice Marshall Fredrick George Hards
1854 - 1855 William Briggs	
1856 - 1878 Mary Reeve	1956 - 1959 Brian Walsh Howarth
1879 - 1879 Harry Smith	

BELL TAP

In common with many large Inns, the Bell also had a public bar, which was situated at the rear of the property in High Street Back. The sign bracket is still in situ.

1871 - 1871 John Church	1908 - H T Applin
1872 - 1896 Ralph Bonass	

BLACK BULL

In 1650 the Black Bull was in the possession of William Tanner. He supplied two barrels of strong beer to William Dyer, late of Ely, and was bringing action against him to recover payment of 7 pounds 4 shillings, which was owing to him. It would seem that Tanner brewed on such a large scale that he was able to supply other licensees. On the trade token that he issued he is described as brewer and not licensee, but he was obviously conducting the business at the Inn in addition to his brewing activities.

In 1807 John Hall, common brewer, paid £420 for the Black Bull, which was described as a messuage or tenement situated near Waterside, *"being now a public house known by the name or sign of the Black Bull"* with barn, granary, stable, yard and garden in the tenure of Phoebe Smith.

On 23rd August 1848 at the annual licensing meeting, Robert Cuttriss had his license suspended for a week, along with his other brothers, to *"allow the magistrates time to consider the most desirable steps to be taken to stop the torrent of vice and infamy consequent upon the irregular and improper manner in which he conducted his house"*, at the adjourned meeting *"the license to Robert Cuttriss Jnr, he having kept a most notoriously wicked house was refused"*.

In 1889 Henry Oakman made an application for the Black Bull to be registered as a common lodging house but was told to wait. When it actually became a lodging house is not certain, but with the increase in barge traffic on the river, there would be considerable demand for overnight accommodation from the bargees. The 1906 Returns of Licensed Houses shows it as having 3 bedrooms for lodgers and one for the landlord, with stabling for 4 horses

The Black Bull was a Hall's pub until the amalgamations of the mid 1900's and held a full alehouse license up until its closure in 1985. The property, 19, Waterside, is now a private residence.

1650 -	William Tanner	1909 - 1910	Richard R Smith
1790 - 1803	George Smith	1911 - 1916	Benjamin Oakman
1804 - 1813	Phoebe Smith	1917 - 1917	Leonard Oakman
1814 - 1815	Thomas Canham	1918 - 1918	Charles H Trimmer
1816 - 1816	James Mann	1919 - 1929	Robert Watman Neal
1817 - 1817	Hannah Dawson	1930 - 1937	Mrs Ellen Neal
1818 - 1847	John Hunt	1937 - 1940	G. Peacock
1848 - 1848	Robert Cuttress	1941 - 1945	Mrs Peacock
1848 - 1864	John Fenn	1946 - 1955	G Peacock
1865 - 1867	Edwin Robert Carter	1955 - 1956	Kenneth Martin Pearce
1868 - 1869	James Cooper	1956 - 1957	Fredrick George Curtis
1870 - 1871	Wybrow Cross	1957 - 1960	Fredrick Joseph Harris
1871 - 1878	Charles Blunt	1961 - 1964	Terence George Chapman
1879 - 1879	Ann Blunt	1965 - 1966	William Ernest Trevillion
1880 - 1883	William Horsley	1967 - 1970	Fredrick Joseph Harris
1884 - 1884	David Eley	1971 - 1973	Harold Lewis Barrett
1885 - 1886	Henry Oakman	1973 - 1976	John Chudyk
1887 - 1887	Wm Oakman	1977 - 1978	Derek Vivian Whiting
1888 - 1894	Henry Oakman	1979 - 1983	John Thomas Wilcox
1895 - 1905	Benjamin Oakman	1983 - 1984	Peter Francis Barnard
1906 - 1908	Alfred Oakman	1985 - 1985	Mark Arther James Curson

BLACK SWAN

The former Black Swan during the 1980's and the site as it is in 2007.

Located at number 2, Station Road, on the corner with Potters Lane, was the Black Swan. The earliest reference to the Black Swan is in 1741 when Ann Chapman was before the Quarter sessions under examination "*saith that on Tuesday last the 15th instant about noon the woman now before me owning her name to be Elizabeth Moreden came to her mother Desborough's house at the Black Swan at Broad Lanes end of Ely and offered a Holland Mobb and calico muslin apron*". For these articles she paid 1/- and they were found to be stolen.

In 1830 Isaac Benton, Carrier, advertised a service to London every Thursday morning.

Landlady Isabella Cranwell was, on 4th December 1842, charged with "*disorderly conduct in her house*" and on August 17th 1855 John Cranwell, who surrendered himself to Sergeant Allpress, was "*fully committed for trial at the ensuing assizes in Cambridge, on a charge of stealing timber, and receiving a large quantity of cement, the property of the Eastern Counties Railway Company*". He was subsequently admitted on bail, himself in £200, and four sureties in the sum of £50 each, which would explain his absence from the licensing list in 1855.

In 1906 the Black Swan was listed as providing 2 bedrooms for the landlords use and 3 available for lodgers, with stabling for 4 horses.

In 1802 John Hall owned the premises and it remained in the Hall family until amalgamation with Cutlack & Harlock in 1930, eventually being closed by East Anglian Breweries in February 1951. The Black Swan held a full alehouse license throughout its history.

After closure of the Black Swan, it was used as a car show room by Graven & Son, which was later taken over by Trigon (Ford) until they closed. The building stood empty until demolition in 1993 and new properties were built on the site in 1995.

1741 -	Mrs Desborough	1864 - 1864	Albert Woodroffe
1790 - 1799	John Cranwell	1865 - 1870	George Cuttriss
1800 - 1801	Thomas Page	1871 - 1875	George Smith
1801 - 1809	William Cranwell	1876 - 1876	Henry Wickes
1809 - 1814	Mary Cranwell	1877 - 1877	Arthur Hall
1815 - 1840	John Cranwell	1878 - 1878	Benton Farr
1841 - 1843	Isabella Cranwell	1879 - 1879	John Saint
1844 - 1855	John Cranwell	1880 - 1882	Charles Berridge
1855 - 1855	Isabella Cranwell	1883 - 1897	George Hawkes Berridge
1856 - 1859	John Cranwell	1898 - 1926	Mrs Emma Berridge
1860 - 1862	Elizabeth Cranwell	1927 - 1942	William Walker
1863 - 1863	Isabella Cranwell	1942 - 1951	Mrs Walker

BRITISH SPORTSMAN

Very little is known of The British Sportsman but it is listed in an 1866 trade directory as being on the South side of Market Street next to the property that became the Sun beer house in 1887. On the 9th September 1869 an application by Edmund Jarvis for a beer house licence was *"refused on the grounds of insufficient ratings"* It is presumed the premises didn't re-open as a beer house. Today the premises is an Indian Restaurant.

1866 - 1866 Thomas Leo   1867 - 1869 Edmund Jarvis

CHEQUERS

The former Chequers Inn during the 1960's and in 2007.

The Chequers, over the centuries, has been known by several different names, the Griffin, the Antelope and the Mitre. As the Griffin it is mentioned in a prosecution against John Gotobed, Braysyer of Ely. John Orwell, gent and John Bert, the younger, Cordwayner, both of Ely, laid information that " *they being in the company of John Gotobed, and talking aboute Religion, the said John Gotobed did say that the Kinge had noe more to doe then these Informants or* himselfe. And that if wee would not be ruled we should be ruled very shortley; and further demaunded of these informants what was the Kinge more than we were". In reply to the charge against him Gotobed said that he came into the house "*of Mr James, called the signe of the Griffin about sixe or seaven of the Clocke in the afternoon*". Orwell called him "*into his Romme and fell upon discourse of Religion and afterwarde he fell in high termes aboute Kings and this examinate said in gods estimacon theire was noe respect of persons if a mans hart was right*". Gotobed denied the treasonable words of which he was accused, but next day William March the magistrate committed him to the "*goale*" This shows that as early as 1642 the revolutionary ideas which were spreading across the country had penetrated the quiet of the Cathedral precincts. The Griffin is mentioned again in an admission to copyhold premises in Steeple Row in 1669. These properties are shown "*next to the tenement called le Griffin*" or in the Latin of the original "*iuxta tenementum nunc vocet' le Griffin*".

A court in 1674 refers back to 1669, when John Poole surrendered "*….unum messuagium sive tenementum cum pertin' scituat' liacen' et existen' in Ely in loco vocat le Anttilope et nunc vocet le Griffin*".
The Antelope, then in the possession of Thomas Swain, was surrendered to Robert Lightfoot of Ely, Esquire in 1725.

In 1784 Francis Harrison was paying a rent of seven pounds five shillings for the inn at the time referred to as "*the Mitre*". Four years later Francis Bagge and Mary, his wife, surrendered to Seth Bull the younger, of Ely, Gentleman "*all that messuage or tenement called or known by the name or sign of the Chequer, late The Mitre and formerly called The Antelope*" then in the occupation of Francis Harrison. Richard Lucas, Potter, in 1789 made a conditional surrender of "*all that messuage divided into two tenements formerly called the Antelope, afterwards the Mitre and since the Chequer, part whereof is still used as an alehouse known by the name of the Chequer*". The two tenements were then in the occupation of Richard Lucas and Francis Harrison.

On 6th April 1839, landlord John Finch was fined £3 with Costs of 14s 10d for "*permitting cards to be played in his house*". John was again in trouble, when at the 1849 annual licensing meeting, he was "*cautioned and informed that his house would be narrowly watched, and if not quietly and respectfully conducted, his license would be withdrawn*". James Cuttriss kept up the family tradition of flouting the law when in April 1858 he appeared on remand, charged by Ralph Hills with "*wilfully cutting a quantity of Osiers*". He was ordered to pay 20s damages £3.3s costs in default of 21 days imprisonment.

By 1875 Messrs Lindsell Brewers of Chatteris owned the Chequers and continued to supply ale to the premises until their takeover by Huntingdon Breweries in 1932 and their merger into East Anglian Breweries in 1950.

In 1906, the Chequers was shown as having 2 bedrooms for the licensee's use, 3 for lodgers and stabling for 16 horses. It closed in February 1958 and held a full ale house license up to its closure

Situated in what is known as Chequer Lane, the property is currently a range of shops.

1642 -	Mr James	1851 - 1852	William Freeman
1650 -	William Seagrave	1853 - 1853	John Onion
1669 -	John Pope	1854 - 1858	James Cuttriss Jnr
1725 -	Thomas Swain	1858 - 1860	Jamess Bright
1725 -	Robert Lightfoot	1861 - 1861	Robert King
1784 - 1793	Francis Harrison	1862 - 1868	Micheal Gibb
1794 - 1800	William Bates	1869 - 1871	Mary Ann Gibb
1801 - 1814	Thomas King	1872 - 1875	Charles Smith
1815 - 1815	John Hills Jnr	1876 - 1895	Robert Jarvis
1816 - 1816	James Dennis	1896 - 1898	Mrs Ann Jarvis
1817 - 1817	Robert Davey	1899 - 1905	Thomas Denton
1817 - 1817	William Topping	1906 - 1914	Isaac William Clark
1818 - 1819	William Thompson	1915 - 1916	William Barham
1820 - 1821	John Segary	1916 - 1929	William Benjamin Fisher
1822 - 1823	W Thurston	1930 - 1948	Alfred Clarke
1823 - 1850	John Finch	1949 - 1958	Edwin Thomas Joyce

CLUB INN

The Club Inn during the 1960's and as it is in 2007.

Situated on the north side of the Market Square, the Club commanded a prominent position.

The earliest reference to the Club Inn may be found in a note in the St. Mary's Churchwardens' Accounts for the year 1610, when William Olecorne was paid "*for carryyinge our quarter bill*". In 1649 the Club Inn is referred to in the Commonwealth Survey of Ely "*Holds all messuage called the Cubb, scituate in the parish of Trinity in Ely in the occ. of... laying between the tenement of the Dean & Chapter late in the tenure of John Tomlynn on the west side and the tenement late of Wm Oldcorns and the tenement Brayes on the east*". In a survey of 1679 the Club is mentioned as "*Mrs Abigail Wagstafe a tenent known by the name of the White Swann in the occupation of Thomas Chaderton abutting upon a tenement of the Deane and Chapter now in the lease to Dorothy Woodham (called the Clubb) toward the east and upon the Market Place towards ye South"*.

This inn was, along with several others in the City, a meeting place for the Governors of the Lands and Possessions of the Poor, i.e. Parsons' Charity, who expended 1s.8d. there in 1690.

In the Cambridge Chronicle of 22nd May 1756 there appeared an advertisement *"Thomas Evans, from the Club Inn, Ely, having filled up the Red Lion in Petty Curry, Cambridge, begs leave to inform his friends and customers that will please to favour him with their company that no care shall be wanting to accommodate them in as genteel a manner as possible"*.

On 29th April 1763 the Trustees for the Turnpike Road from Ely to Downham Market met *"at the house of John Collison known by the sign of the clubb in Ely"*.

There was a sale at the houses of James Robinson *"being the sign of the Club in Ely"* in August 1758. In 1764 the Ely Trinity Jury List names John Collison as the inn holder, presumably of the Club, for in 1786 Widow Collison is paying a rent of £10 at the Club Inn.

Following the Ely and Littleport riots in 1816, the citizens of Ely held a meeting at the Club Inn to agree a petition be presented on behalf of the prisoners.

In 1824 Carriers were leaving from the Club every Thursday for Newmarket, and on Monday, Thursday and Saturday for Soham. At this time John Barnard was landlord and during his occupation various carriers left the Club for Littleport, Newmarket, Soham and Wisbech. In 1850 Carriers were leaving on Thursdays for Earith, Mildenhall and Welney. Carriers continued to leave the inn on Thursday, market day, to the end of the 1800s.

William Scales, landlord, was on 15th August 1842, charged with *"keeping his house open"*.

When The Club Inn was put up for auction in 1852 by Nash & Co of Royston, it was shown in the auction catalogue as Lot 25 and listed as *"A very capital and Well-Accustomed HOUSE, containing Bar, Tap Room, Kitchen, Parlours, Dining and Club Rooms, Nine Bed Rooms, Cellarage, Yard, Range of Stabling to accommodate about Forty Horses, Coach House, and Back Entrance towards the Cattle Market ... This House, which is most respectably tenanted, must, from its central situation, always command a good trade"*. It sold for 940 guineas to Ebenezer W Harlock, brewer of Ely.

In 1892 Friendly Societies held their meetings at the Club: The Rock of Hope and the Ancient Order of Foresters.

The Returns of Licensed Houses of 1906 shows the Club as having 4 bedrooms for the landlord's use and 3 for lodgers with stabling for 16 horses and 5 vehicles.

The Ely Amateur Boxing Club used the Club Inn from 1937 until 1940 when it was dissolved for the duration of the war, with training nights on Wednesdays. Between 1947 and 1953 it was also home to the Ely & District Motorcycle Club.

The Club held a full alehouse license and remained a Harlock's house until the takeovers of the mid 1900's. It was closed by Watney Mann in 1975, although the license wasn't surrendered until 1976. Following its closure and after a long campaign, chiefly by The Ely Society, to retain the building fronting onto the Market Square, the yard was redeveloped and forms part of what is now Cloisters shopping area. The old yard and stables were where the public toilets are now. On the panel between the top windows the words "The Club Hotel" can still be made out through the paint.

1679 -	Dorothy Woodham	1908 -1908 Mrs Elizabeth Allen
1756 -	Thomas Evans	1909 - 1910 Thomas Henry William Keates
1763 - 1766	John Collison	1911 - 1913 Harry Stockbridge
1767 - 1781	Ann Spenceley	1914 - 1938 Mrs Laura Stockbridge
1786 -	Widow Collison	1939 - 1941 Karl Erik Firman
1790 - 1794	George Hardy	1941 - 1945 Muriel Edith Firman
1795 - 1807	George Read	1946 - 1953 Karl Erik Firman
1808 - 1812	Catherine Read	1954 - 1958 Alan Underwood McMinn
1813 - 1815	William Botson	1958 - 1965 Stanley Roy Dewey
1816 - 1822	John Hawkins	1966 - 1966 John Allen Dolby
1823 - 1828	John Barnard	1967 - 1967 Kenneth Frank Howard
1829 - 1830	John Anderson	1968 - 1968 Leonard Jack Dawkes
1831 - 1831	John Seggary,	1968 - 1968 Kenneth Peter Brown
1832 - 1835	John Cole	1969 - 1972 Edward Kendle Thackeray
1836 - 1836	William Thorpe	1972 - 1974 Leslie Cyril Munt
1837 - 1840	Robert Cuttress	1974 - 1975 John Edward Lemmon
1841 - 1849	William Scales	1975 - 1976 Geoffrey Eric Minnett
1850 - 1874	William Roan	
1875 - 1907	Albert Cosyn Allen	

COACH AND HORSES

On the west side of Broad Street was found the Coach & Horses, though it never had stabling facilities for coaches or horses! It did however carry a full alehouse license allowing it to serve beers, wines and liquors and in 1906 was listed as having 4 bedrooms for lodgers and 2 for the licensee's family.

The Cathedral Authorities had right of way through a passageway belonging to the property which allowed goods to be brought by barrow up from the river along Hythe Lane, formerly Little Lane, across Broad Street and through to the Dean's meadow and on to the Cathedral.

On 2nd March 1832 a charge was bought against "*William Frommet, landlord of Coach & Horses in Ely for disorderly conduct*" and no doubt this led to him not renewing his license that year.

An auction advisement of June 1838, listed Lot 4 as "*All that well accustomed Free Public House, known by the sign of The Coach and Horses, situate in Broad Street, in Ely, now occupied by Mr James Barratt, together with an excellent and very productive Garden, well planted with choice fruit trees, as now occupied by Mr Luke Cornwall*".

In 1859 landlord William Dewey was charged on 2 counts of "*deficient measures*" and fined 5s with 12s 6d costs.

In 1874 the owner was a King's Lynn brewer, Eyre & Co, then in 1876 Fredrick Bailey of Cambridge had taken the Inn, followed by Charles Armstrong in 1890, finally Morgan's Brewery Co Ltd, of Norwich, owned the Coach & Horses from 1898 up to its closure by 1916. Today the property is in use as a Chinese Takeaway outlet.

The former Coach and Horses in the 1960's.

1805 - 1820 Edward Bromfield	1866 - 1871 William Willson Baker
1821 - 1823 Thomas Tolworthy	1872 - 1873 Henry Cropley
1824 - 1830 John Jarman	1874 - 1875 Michael Collen
1831 - 1832 William Fromet	1876 - 1898 William Woods
1832 - 1832 Thomas Benton	1899 - 1900 George Alfred Bull
1833 - 1835 John Barnard	1900 - 1903 Samual Cox
1836 - 1840 James Barratt	1904 - 1905 Frank Peck
1841 - 1849 Philip Rickwood	1906 - 1910 Charles G Griffin
1850 - 1856 James Barrett	1911 - 1912 George Spendelow
1857 - 1857 Richard Searle	1913 - 1913 Charles G Griffin
1858 - 1858 Thomas Hutchcraft	1914 - 1914 Fredrick Hugh Firth
1859 - 1865 William Dewey	1915 - 1915 William King

COOPERS' ARMS

Situated on Waterside, the Coopers' Arms no doubt took its name from the trade employed at the near-by brewery. It was owned by William Cranwell in 1792 until 1796 when Thomas Page acquired it, then in 1803 John Hall became the owner and it remained with the Hall family up to the amalgamation with Cutlack & Harlock finally becoming East Anglian Breweries Ltd.

In the 1906 Return of Licensed Houses it was listed as having 2 bedrooms for the family use, 2 bedrooms for lodgers and stabling for two horses.

The Coopers' Arms after its closure and the properties that occupy the site in 2007.

The "Coopers" was one of several pubs to run a fishing club and had fishing rights along the Cresswells, this continued after the pub closed and the Coopers' Fishing Club is still in existence today where it has fishing rights just beyond the railway bridge towards Littleport.

In common with many pubs in the inter war years the Coopers' Arms ran a Slate Club for its regulars. It was licensed as an alehouse until early 1950 when the license was swapped with the Red, White & Blue's beer house license. The Coopers' then traded as a beer house until closure on the 4th January 1955 by East Anglian Breweries Ltd. The building was demolished in 1972 and a new property now stands on its site at 42, Waterside.

1792 - 1804 Thomas Vail
1805 - 1808 Ann Vail
1809 - 1809 Henry Parsons
1810 - 1833 Mary Parsons
1834 - 1836 John Raby
1837 - 1856 Francis Cropley
1857 - 1857 Mary Cropley
1858 - 1884 John Frost

1885 - 1895 Mrs Susan Frost
1896 - 1896 Alfred Dunham
1897 - 1901 John Dunham
1902 - 1907 George Martin
1908 - 1937 George Suckling
1937 - 1941 David William Harding
1941 - 1954 John William Jenkins

CROMWELL ARMS

Situated in St Mary's Street next to St Mary's Parish Church, the one time home of Oliver Cromwell was from 1843 to 1871 owned by Joseph Rushbrook, who opened it as The Cromwell Arms Inn and also started a small brewery to provide his customers with "*Rushbrook's Home Brewed Ale*". Rushbrook could only sell beer, as on his application for a full license to sell spirits, he was refused by the local magistrates. Between 1850 and 1862 he made 11 unsuccessful applications! Thereupon he set up a sign over his door painted by local artist John Toombs, the Town Cryer. "*This signboard shews, in caricature, the members of the bench of magistrates Dean Peacock and the Reverend George Hall, minor canon and J.P. A grandfather clock stands in the background showing the time as well after closing hours, indicating that the roistering was being conducted after the time permitted by law. This caused such a sensation in Ely that the Council ordered the removal of the sign*". This signboard survives and is sometimes exhibited in Cromwell House. Joseph Rushbrook eventually secured a full spirit license on 26th February 1863. In 1869 the Cromwell Arms was put up for auction and was described as "*All that old established, well built, Freehold Hotel, called the Cromwell Arms situate in Saint Mary's in Ely, containing 2 cellars, store-room, bar, smokey, large dining-room, large kitchen, pantry, Tap-room and 6 bedrooms. Also All that 3 quarter brewery, malt-chamber, stables, gig-house and other outbuildings, yard and capital garden well planted and walled in....*". A bid was received for £690 but was not accepted. Rushbrook became bankrupt and in 1871 the property was mortgaged and conveyed to Henry Lawrence.

From 1905 the house became St Mary's Vicarage and remained so until it was sold to the East Cambridgeshire District Council, then in 1990 it opened as Ely's Tourist Information Centre.

1843 - 1871   Joseph Rushbrook

CROWN AND ANCHOR

The site of the former Crown and Anchor in 2007.

The Crown and Anchor once stood at what is now 68, St Mary's Street and held a full alehouse license until its surrender in 1932 when the pub closed. Between 1826 and 1871 it was also sometimes known as the Anchor.

In Nash & Co's auction of Inns and public houses in 1852, Lot 29 was the Crown & Anchor and described as "*Brick and Tile well-accustomed HOUSE, containing Two Parlours, Tap Room, Kitchen, Dairy, Cellar, Five Bed Rooms, YARD, GARDEN, Stables, and Two Pantiled Lodges; together with Back Entrance into Engine Road*". It was sold for 310 guineas to Thomas Legge, brewer of Ely.

On August 26th 1858 John Ellis appeared before the magistrates charged under the weights and measures act of "*giving 2 false measures*", the information was withdrawn on payment of 5s 6d cost.

The 1906 Return of Licensed Houses showed the Crown & Anchor as having 4 bedrooms for lodgers, 1 for the licensee's family with stabling for 16 horses and 6 vehicles. Between 1900 and 1922 Lowe and Sennitt advertised a carriers service from the Crown and Anchor to Stretham daily except Thursdays.

1799 - 1812 Nathaniel Cock	1862 - 1864 Joseph Rich
1813 - 1818 William Ellingham	1865 - 1871 Robert Marsh
1819 - 1822 John Finch	1872 - 1878 Thomas Bibby
1823 - 1824 Timothy Russell	1879 - 1884 John Evan Ellis
1825 - 1825 No Return	1885 - 1889 James Beaumont
1826 - 1858 John Ellis	1890 - 1905 Mrs Ellen Lydia Beaumont
1859 - 1861 Elizabeth Balls	1906 - 1932 Joseph S Nightingale

CROWN

The Crown, 2007.

There are records of an alehouse called the Crown in the Parish of St Mary dating back to 1790. It is believed that the license lapsed in 1847 and when it reopened, it was licensed as a beer house. It became another of Nash & Co's pubs to be put up for auction in 1852 and was listed as Lot 30, a Beer house and described as " *A Brick and Tile HOUSE, containing Four lower Rooms, Cellar, Three Bed Rooms, YARD, GARDEN, Pump, Lodges, etc*". The property sold for 266 guineas to Ely brewer, Henry Hall.

In 1854 and 1861 John Nicolas, who was a Greenwich pensioner, applied for a full (alehouse) license but was refused. On 19th August 1869 landlord Thomas Peel was prosecuted for *"Have open for the sale of beer before 12 ½"* and fined17/6 with 12/6 costs, when he applied for his license to be renewed on 25th August 1869 it was refused *"on the grounds that the house was of a disorderly character"* however, at the licensing meeting on 28th August 1873 his application was allowed and he continued trading.

The Crown was typical in design of many of the smaller beer houses, the Tap-room was on the left of the passageway that ran from the front door to the back of the property, the room to the right was the landlord's sitting room, up stairs there were 3 bedrooms, 2 for the licensee's use and one for lodgers. There was no rear access therefore no stabling was available and all barrels and crates would have been carried through the house to the back yard. The Crown remained with the Hall family until 1930, when they joined forces with Cutlack & Harlock. The premises closed as a beer house and the license surrendered on 8th February 1957 under East Anglian Breweries Ltd. Today the old Crown Inn at 46, Silver Street is a private residence.

1790 - 1793 J Sharman	1873 - 1873 Thomas Peel
1793 - 1793 William Sharman	1874 - 1875 William Peel
1794 - 1800 Sarah Sharman	1876 - 1880 Maria Peel
1801 - 1830 Thomas Day	1881 - 1894 William Pearson
1831 - 1834 Hannah Day	1895 - 1900 Mrs Maria Pearson
1835 - 1843 William Elwood	(formally Peel)
1844 - 1846 James Mayle	1901 - 1901 Ebenezer Dewey
1847 - 1849 No return	1902 - 1903 George Lock
1850 - 1864 John Nicholas	1904 - 1906 Harry Trevers
1866 - 1866 Mrs M Myles	1907 - 1909 Alfred Bradnam
1867 - 1869 Thomas Peel	1910 - 1914 George James Pope
1869 - 1872 No license granted	1915 - 1942 Harry Trevers

CROWN INN

The second establishment in Ely to be named the Crown Inn was situated at what was 49, Station Road and was no doubt built to capture trade from the newly opened railway line, which reached Ely in 1845. It originally held a full alehouse license, which it kept up until closure.

In 1852 Nash & Co, the Royston brewers sold off their business and the Crown was put up for auction. In the sales catalogue Lot 31 was described as *"A newly-erected Brick and Slate HOUSE, containing Tap Room, Front and Back Parlours, Bar, Wash-house, and SIX Bed Rooms, large YARD, GARDEN, and extensive Range of Brick and Slate STABLES, Lofts etc."* and *" These Premises are all newly built, well Tenanted and from their excellent situation command a good trade"*. The Crown was sold to Ebenezer William Harlock for 545 guineas.

The Crown Inn during the 1950's

    The Crown's first landlord, Thomas Marsh, was charged on the 23 September 1859 with having 2 counts of "*deficient weights and measures*" and fined 7s 6d with 12s 6d costs. Whilst Thomas Morley was licensee he was caught twice for "*keeping his house open for the sale of beer*" at prohibited times during 1889, firstly on 14th March for which he had to pay the court costs and secondly on 2nd August for which he was fined 11/6 with 15/6 costs. In 1896 James Maltpress was no better, as he was charged that on 1st November "*he open his house for the sale of intoxicating liquors contrary to the licensing acts*" and was fined 40/- with £1-10-1 costs and his license endorsed.

    Between 1869 and 1875 Clements advertised a daily carriers service from the Crown to Soham. During the tenure of Wm Harding and J E Webster, horse slaughtering was also a business carried out on the premises.

    The 1906 Returns of Licensed Houses shows it had 2 bedrooms for the use of the licensee and 6 bedrooms for lodgers with stabling for 9 horses and 6 vehicles. After Ebenezer Harlock bought the Crown it remained in the Harlock family and subsequent mergers until its closure in February 1964 by Watney Mann. The building was demolished, and today, an engineering firm occupies the site.

1847 - 1871 Thomas Marsh
1872 - 1872 Elizabeth Marsh
1873 - 1873 Michael Collen
1874 - 1884 Joseph Eagle
1885 - 1885 Richard Glynn
1886 - 1896 Thomas Morley
1896 - 1902 James Maltpress
1903 - 1909 William Harding
1910 - 1910 Mary Harding

1911 - 1916 John Edward Webster
1917 - 1920 John Thomas Taylor
1920 - 1926 Percival Harmer
1926 - 1929 Francis Joseph Conroy
1930 - 1945 Harold Cuthbert Childs
1946 - 1949 James Dolby
1950 - 1957 Horace Crouch
1957 - 1962 Henry Bodger
1962 - 1964 George Lewis Gay

CUTTER

The Cutter on Coronation Day 1937.

Probably the best known of Ely's pubs is the Cutter, situated in a picturesque location by the river Ouse. Opened in 1830 to take advantage of the increased river trade due to the opening of the new "river cut" in the same year. Originally the property was built as a pair of maltsters cottages for the nearby granary. The property ran from Broad Street down to the river's edge and had its own brewery.

On 13th April 1837 the Cutter was put up for auction and was described as " *Very Desirable Estate at Ely, To Merchants, Maltsters and Brewers", Consisting of a capital Brick Dwelling House, with Counting House and other offices and yard, Garden, Stables, and Coach-House attached. Also an extensive Malting, with 13 quarter Steep, and with large Barley Chamber about it, Malt-Kiln, and Malt Chamber, and Granaries over the Maltings, extending along the whole length of the building. Also a small but convenient Brewery adjoining, fitted up with 13 Barrel Copper, 6 quarter Mash-Tub, hand mashing machine, and other suitable utensils, making a very complete plant and with Store Rooms adjoining. Also a capital and well accustomed Inn, called THE CUTTER, adjoining the private dwelling-house, with stabling for 14 Horses and other convenient out-buildings, Also a Lime Kiln adjoining lodger, Also a Dwelling House used as a Tap to the CUTTER INN, situate in Broad Street, with excellent cellar, liquor shop, and out buildings, the whole connected with the Cutter Inn by a good Yard and Garden. The above premises are in excellent repair, part being newly built, and are worthy of attention of Merchants, Maltsters and Brewers, being in Full Trade and situate at Ansdale Quay, in Ely adjoining the river Ouse, and lying on the main line of navigation between Cambridge and Lynn, extending from the river to Broad Street*".

It was advertised for auction 5 times between 1837 and 1842 when John Torley became landlord. It was un-licensed and presumably vacant for 1841.

The Cutter's Brewing Plant was up for auction on 1st February 1842 and described as " *A Capital Brewing Plant, consisting of 13 Barrel Copper with furnace, Brass cock and fittings complete, Hot and Cold Liquor Pumps, Six quarter Mash tub, with Cast-iron false bottom and Mashing machine, Three Coolers with brass cocks, working vat, Hop Back, Three cleaning troughs, Two New 50 Barrel Vats, with Brass Cocks Stayer and Spouts etc. The above will be sold in such lots as may be agreed on the time of sale and, for ready money*".

Mr Torley hadn't been in occupation long before he was charged on the 15th August 1842 with "*keeping his house open*" during unlicensed hours. The Cutter and Cutter Tap were advertised for auction again on 11th September 1847.

A report in the Cambridge Chronicle of the Annual Licensing meeting on 25th August 1848 stated "*At the annual general meeting held on Wednesday last, James Dill, landlord of the Cutter Inn, Ely, on applying for his license was refused, and the same suspended on account of the disorderly state of the Cutter Tap, it appeared that the tap is kept by his servant, Robert Cuttriss, formally landlord of The Bull public house, notorious for the noise and disturbances which used to take place there, until the magistrates refused to renew the license, when he left, and was last year placed by Dill in charge of the Cutter Tap, but Dill fearing the magistrates would refuse a renewal of his own license, very shrewdly closed the Tap a week or two previous to the licensing day, in 1848, when on obtaining the same, Cuttriss was a few days afterwards installed tap keeper, since then it appears the house has been conducted very badly, on which account the magistrates, determined not to grant the license while Cuttriss remained*". Mr William Holland became licensee until 1849 when Mr Dill resumed the license, during this time the Cutter was yet again advertised for auction together with the Cutter Tap, Granaries, Lime Kiln etc.

At the Magistrates Court on 6th February 1852 "*John and Jonas Newman of Ely, labourers, apprehended by P.C. Hill and Howitt on suspicion of stealing a large copper from the unoccupied premises of the Cutter Inn in Ely, the property of H.R.Evans Esq. of Brighton. Remanded until Thursday, when John Newman was committed for trial at the session and Jonas Newman discharged*".

Although the Cutter initially had its own brewery by 1860 it was being supplied by Eyre's Brewery of Kings Lynn, however, by 1875 William Cutlack, brewer of Littleport, had purchased the Inn and was obviously supplying the ales.

During Richard Morton Hill's tenure he was twice before the magistrates for offences against his license, firstly he was charged that on the 20th December 1868 "*Having his house open after 11am on Sunday*" for which he paid 6/6 costs and secondly that on 21st February 1873 "*Permitting prostitutes to associate in his house*" for which he was fined 50/- with 1/2/6 costs.

The 1906 Returns of Licensed Houses lists the Cutter as having 3 bedrooms for the landlord's use and 6 for lodgers with stabling for 2 horses and 10 vehicles.

The Cutter was one of several pubs in Ely to run a fishing club and was popular with anglers from the Midlands and West Yorkshire. Along with many pubs of the time the Cutter ran a Slate Club for its regulars during the years between the two Wars. The Cutter Sports and Social Club hosted a dinner "*to the repatriated Eleans of the Cambridgeshire Regiment*", who served in the 2nd World War, on 16th November 1945.

By 1960, the Cutter had become a Steward & Patteson house, then passing to Watney Mann; it is now in the hands of Inntrepeneur Inns. The Cutter held a full alehouse license, which also covered the Cutter Tap.

After a refurbishment in 2006, the popular riverside inn continues to prosper today.

The Cutter summer 2006.

1830 - 1840 Morley Wright Cutlack	1884 - 1904 Mrs Mary Ann Hill
1842 - 1842 John Torley	1905 - 1929 Thomas Thompson Hill
1843 - 1843 No return	1929 - 1962 Kenneth Horace Wenn
1844 - 1845 Robert Denton	1962 - 1968 John William Jenkins
1846 - 1848 James Dill	1969 - 1976 Lewis Sidney David Rich
1848 - 1848 William Smith Holland	1977 - 1984 Richard Archibald Davies
1849 - 1851 James Dill	1985 - 1991 Keith John Blackwell
1852 - 1853 Thomas Pamplin	1992 - 1998 Sheila Blackwell
1854 - 1854 William Pratt Gotobed	1999 - 2002 Timothy John Smith
1855 - 1858 John Bird	2002 - 2004 Lynsey Ann Cockram
1859 - 1865 William Cave Cranwell	2005 - 2005 Steven Baker
1866 - 1866 William Hill	2005 - 2005 John Francis Blick
1867 - 1867 Charles Miller	2006 - Curr. Steve Haslam
1868 - 1883 Richard Morton Hill	

CUTTER TAP

The Cutter Tap in 1937 on Coronation Day and the site as it is in 2007.

Situated at 45 Broad Street, next to the Three Blackbirds. The Cutter Tap carried the same license as the Cutter Inn

DOG AND GUN

Mrs Dann, on the right, next to the cart, is handing a customer a pint of Hall's ale.

The Dog and Gun is believed to have opened in 1858 and was owned by Henry Hall, and it remained in the Hall family until the merger of 1930. It only held a beer house license and could provide 3 bedrooms for lodgers with stabling for 2 horses

Robert Joselyn was charged on the 2nd June 1860 with "*having in his possession, 5 measures intended to represent pints and another measure, a half pint, all of which were deficient*" he was fined 7s 6d with 12s 6d costs.

The former Dog and Gun as it is in 2007.

After only a year as landlord, William Dann, who had been a Colour Sergeant in the Army, died in May 1900 leaving the running of the pub to his wife, son and daughter. Tragedy struck again on 12th April 1918 when their son, Thomas Charles Dann, was killed in action during the Great War. He was aged 23 and was serving as a Private in the 40th Machine Gun Corps at the time.

In March 1970 the owners, Watney Mann, closed the Dog and Gun. The property was sold off and after major alterations; it now forms part of two private residences, numbers 80 and 82 Cambridge Road.

1858 - 1865 Robert Joselyn
1867 - 1870 Edward Kimpton
1871 - 1871 Vacant
1872 - 1894 William Newell
1895 - 1898 James Gillson

1899 - 1900 William Henry Dann
1900 - 1932 Mrs Alice Rebecca Dann
1933 - 1958 Ralph Richard Moon
1959 - 1962 Minnie Rebecca Moon
1962 - 1970 Horace Jones

DOLPHIN

An illustration of the Dolphin circa 18th century and the former Dolphin in 2007 with the Victorian extension onto the High Street.

The Dolphin Inn stood on the corner of the High Street and what is now Dolphin Lane, and it dates back to at least the 17th Century. In 1641 King Charles I revised the Corporation of Parsons' Charity, or the Lands and Possessions of the Poor of Ely that had been founded by Thomas Parsons in the 15th century. The finances of the Charity seem to have been in a rather confused state so the King set up a commission to look into its affairs. He called upon Tho. Symond, Tho. Duckett, and Dudley Pope, citizens of Ely, to make a personal appearance before his commission. This took place "*att the signe of the Dolphin in Ely att or upon the ffive and twenteth of this instant January betweene the howers of eight and nyne of the clocke in the morning of the same daye then and there to produce before us a true account of all monyes, fines, rents and proffitts by you and eny of you and your predecessors ffeoffees received out of the lands given by one Parsons for the benefit of the inhabitants of Ely.....*" In addition to the Bishop and other high ecclesiastics, a number of laymen of importance also attended, including Oliver Cromwell who was then residing in Ely.

In 1650 William Segrave was prosecuted for "*keepinge disorder in his house upon the Sabboth day, by drinckinge and singinge Caveleire songs*"

The Lord Bishop of Ely in 1686 held his dinner "*at Mr. Smeggergill's, who now keeps the Dolphin Inn*". It seems as though Mr. Smeggergill was not an ideal landlord for the complaint was made that "*his ill manner has not deserved soe good encouragement*".

One of the periodical disturbances, which gave rise to riots in the Littleport area, occurred in 1689. The magistrates repaired to the Dolphin, where they issued a warrant for the arrest of the rioters and expended three shillings and sixpence at the inn.

The Governors of Parsons' Charity record that at their meeting in 1662 they *"expended with Mr. Mallabar at the Dollphin one shilling and sixpence."* On 3rd May 1675 the Governors summoned their members to *"meete together at the house in Ely called the Dolphin"* to elect *"Peeter Gunning, Lord Bishop of Ely"* to be one of their number. The Parsons' Charity account book records the transfer in 1727 to Samuel Cole of Ely, Gent, of *"one piece of Waste in the Beest Market called the pump yard, lying next the Dolphin Inn, now in the occupation of Henry Nunn"*. Henry was succeeded at the Dolphin by his son William, who when he died in 1761 bequeathed to his widow Lucy *"all my messuage or tenement wherein I now dwell, situate in or near the Market Place in Ely commonly called the Dolphin Inn with all and singular the shops, cellars, yards, stables, brewhouse etc"*. On 22nd May 1793 Lucy Nunn surrendered the property to John Harlock, who was admitted in April of the next year. It consisted of *"all that piece of waste laying over against the cross in the Beef Market, called the Pump Yard, on the east of the Dolphin, containing in length forty feet and in breadth at the end eight feet and at the south end four feet, by the yearly rent of one penny"*. When John Harlock made his will in 1794 he bequeathed to his son William *"a messuage called the Dolphin "*. John Harlock's will was not proved until 1816, when William was admitted to the property.

Carriers' carts from Cambridge to Lynn were calling at the inn in 1823: Marsh & Swann's Waggons to Cambridge every Thursday and twice a week to Lynn. In 1839 James Beaumont who had been landlord since 1825 was entertaining Marsh & Swann's Fly vans *"Every morning (Sunday excepted) at seven; their waggons every Monday at two"*. In 1848 William Laws was visited every Monday and Thursday by "*the carrier*" from Hilgay.

Landlord Jeffrey Palmer was charged on 10th February 1878 with "*selling to a child under 16 years of age and permitting drunkenness*" for which he was fined £1 with 17/6 costs. On 21st March 1897 William Hudson was charged, "*with serving Alfred Miller when drunk with intoxicating liquor given him being a traveller*" which no doubt led to his license not being renewed the following year.

In 1906 the inn provided its landlord with 5 bedrooms but none for lodgers, though there was stabling for 5 horses and 5 vehicles.

The Dolphin carried an alehouse license up to its closure and was owned and supplied by E W Harlock's brewery from 1875. It remained a Harlock's house until the mergers of the mid 1900s, eventually being closed on 1st September 1965 by Steward & Patteson. The property continued to sell wines & spirits after its closure as a pub, as various wine companies, including Peter Dominic and Threshers have owned it.

Today you can still enjoy a drink in the Dolphin as in 2005 it became Starbucks Coffee Shop.

1650 -	William Segrave	1876 - 1876	Jeremiah Lee
1662 -	Mr Mallaber	1877 - 1878	Jeffrey Palmer
1686 -	Mr Smeggergill	1879 - 1879	Richard Wise
1702 - 1727	Henry Nunn	1879 - 1879	Thomas Yates
- 1761	William Nunn	1879 - 1895	John Newstead
1761 - 1790	Lucy Nunn	1896 - 1897	William Hudson
1791 - 1801	Thomas Barnard	1898 - 1912	John Newstead
1802 - 1807	Elizabeth Barnard	1913 - 1935	Percy Charles Newstead
1808 - 1824	William Gray	1935 -	Fredrick Bevan
1825 - 1844	James Beaumont	1937 - 1944	Percival Harmer
1845 - 1845	Sarah Beaumont	1944 - 1945	Robert John Aston
1846 - 1866	William Laws	1946 - 1957	Frank Edward Robinson
1867 - 1872	Joseph Rich	1957 - 1965	Sidney Lovell Rains
1873 - 1875	George Mather		

DUKE OF WELLINGTON

The Duke of Wellington a few years after closure and the site in 2007.

The Duke of Wellington was situated at number 35, Newnham Street on the junction with Nutholt lane and was licensed as a beer house. In 1851 W Harlock owned the property and supplied the ale. It remained in the Harlock family until 1907, when they merged with Cutlack's brewery.

The earliest available reference to the Duke of Wellington is a listing in a trade directory of 1847 where Samuel Spring is listed as a beer retailer and butcher.

Landlord Thomas Blowfield had not long taken over the Duke of Wellington when he was charged with "*keeping house open for the sale of beer on 1st August 1875*" he was fined £2 for the privilege.

In the 1906 Return of Licensed Houses, it was listed as having 1 bedroom for the licensee's family and 4 for lodgers with stabling for 16 horses and 3 vehicles and required a urinal!

The Duke of Wellington is believed to have closed 1957 whilst in East Anglian Breweries ownership.

1847 - 1853	Samuel Spring	1884 - 1909	Elizabeth Blowfield
1864 - 1870	Jacob Poulson	1910 - 1914	John William Clayton
1871 - 1871	John Moulson Cox	1915 - 1937	Charles Henry Beezley
1872 - 1873	Thomas James Cornish	1938 - 1941	Hannah Beezley
1874 - 1874	Richard Chapman	1941 - 1956	John Beezley
1875 - 1884	Thomas Blowfield	1956 - 1957	Emily Beezley

DUKE OF YORK

The building that was once the Duke Of York Inn as it is in 2007.

Situated on the corner of Market Place and Fore hill, opposite the Three Cups was the Duke Of York. One of Ely's lost ancient inns it dates back to the 17th century. Reference to it was made in 1679 to the Duke of York, "*High Row Ward, North Side, West the Bullock Market*" Manor of Ely Porta. The property survives today as a Travel Agent.

EAGLE AND LAMB

Along Cambridge Road at what was number 31, once stood the Eagle and Lamb public house and situated behind was the Eagle brewery.

In 1848 William Scales purchased a parcel of land on Cambridge Road, which the Eagle and Lamb would be built on, for £400. It was certainly open in 1851, as the magistrates received an application for a full license on 27th August from William Scales, of the Eagle and Lamb beer house, which was refused.

In the 24th December 1853 edition of the Cambridge Chronicle an advert was placed for the auction of the premises, described as " *Valuable Freehold Dwelling House, used as Public House and a Newly erected Brewery. To Be Sold By Auction at the Bell Inn 12th January 1854 called the Eagle situate on the Cambridge Road Ely. The entirely New four-quarter Brewing Plant fitted up with every convenience for carrying on an extensive trade*". Presumably it did not attract any bids as the premises were advertised for auction again on 24th August 1854. A notice in the Cambridge Chronicle of 1855 reported "*Death At Ely, January 8^{th,} aged 42, Mr William Scales, late of the Eagle Brewery*".

The site of the former Eagle and Lamb in 2007.

It is assumed the property remained unlicensed from 1855 to 1856 as on 7th April 1856, Richard Porter, freehold Brewer, purchased the site for £700 and ran his business from there until he sold the premises to Morgan's Brewery Co. Ltd. on 24th June 1889 for £1250. Morgan's closed the brewery part of the business in 1902 but used the site as a distribution depot until 11th May 1920 when Ely brewers A&B Hall purchased the premises for £5000.

A trade directory of 1867 listed Samuel Richard as a beer retailer and ginger beer manufacturer. In 1869 a Carriers service was advertised from the Eagle and Lamb to Cambridge on Wednesdays and Saturdays.

The 1906 Return of Licensed Houses listed 3 bedrooms for the landlord's use and 1 for lodgers though there was no stabling provided. The Eagle and Lamb carried a beer house license throughout its history and was closed on 30th September 1932. The public house was demolished in the winter of 1987/88 and the site is now the entrance to a small cul-de-sac, part of the brewery building survives, as it was converted into a private dwelling

1851 - 1854 William Scales	1906 - 1906 Cornelius T Ellwood
1867 - 1872 Samuel Richard	1906 - 1906 Edward J Fogg
1873 - 1889 Charles Scarr	1907 - 1914 Jonathan Wilson
1890 - 1891 Harry Berry	1915 - 1917 Henry John Fordham
1891 - 1892 Albert Stoney	1918 - 1921 Walter Gray
1892 - 1898 George Cross	1922 - 1922 Robert Mortiss
1899 - 1904 Mrs Vines Cross	1923 - 1932 Thomas. Lucas
1905 - 1905 Walter Waston	

ELEPHANT AND CASTLE

Little is known of this Inn but it is shown on Bidwell's map of 1851. The Elephant & Castle stood in the northern corner of Bugs Hill (Cambridge Road) and Smock Mill Alley (Barton Road). Reference to it is also found in trade directories.

It is believed that it is the same Aaron Layton, who was one of the Littleport rioters originally sentenced to hang in 1816, but due to public outcry the sentence was reduced to one year in Ely Gaol.

Today nothing remains of the Inn and new properties occupy the site.

1847 - 1851 Aaron Layton   1858 - John Giles

FIRST AND LAST

Very little is know of the First & Last, but it was indeed, the first and last pub on the Lynn Road. Reference to it is made in the 1851 Valuation List and lists it between the Tinker beer house, later the Rifleman's Arms, and an area known as the Oakery. It is believed that it was located in what became the Tinker's car park, which is now the site of 150 Lynn Road. It was licensed as a beer house and there is no reference to it after 1851.

1847 - 1851   George Finch

FIVE BELLS

The Five Bells was situated in "*a place commonly called the Butchery and near Gaol Street, in Ely*" which is now referred to as Butchers Row, and had closed as an Inn by the mid 1800s. A notice in the Cambridge Chronicle advertising the property's auction, to be held at the Lamb Inn, Ely on Friday 28th May 1847 described the property as " *A valuable Property, consisting of a large brick built messuage with 4 good rooms and a large attic, yard, and cartage, and a pump of most excellent water, and now in the occupation of H R Evans. These premises were formally an Inn called The Five Bells*".

FOUNTAIN

In 1848 Joseph Rushbrook (also of the Cromwell Arms) acquired the property as it was described in a mortgage as "*newly erected*" on the "*site of an old messuage or tenement heretofore divided into Three Tenements......*". It was at this time that the Fountain acquired its name.

When James Rushbrook, who was a son of Joseph, was landlord the ale would have undoubtedly been supplied from Joseph Rushbrook's Cromwell House brewery until 1869, when the Fountain was put up for auction, and described as "*All that newly built Brick and Slate, Freehold Beer House, called the "Fountain" situate at the corner of Silver Street in Ely, with a frontage of 57 feet 6 inches, containing cellar, tap-room, parlour, and kitchen, large dining or club room, and 4 chambers, with yard, stables, and out buildings, thereto belonging....*", Littleport brewer, William Cutlack bought the property. James Rushbrook made 5 applications for a full (alehouse) license between 1851 and 1862 but each was refused. The Fountain was originally licensed as a beer house but in 1870 an application for a full alehouse license was made by Alfred Smith, which was duly granted.

The Fountain during the 1960's.

Between 1869 and 1875 Elsdon the carriers, advertised a service from the Fountain to Soham.

In 1906 it was shown to have 4 bedrooms for the licensee's family with stabling for 3 horses and 1 vehicle. During the World Wars it ran, like many others, a Slate Club for its regulars.

The Fountain continued as a Cutlack's house until 1908 when the firm merged with that of F.L.Harlock. After passing through the various mergers and takeovers of the mid to late 1900s it closed in 1995 whilst owned by Pubmaster.

In 1996 the Fountain re-opened and is still open for trade today as a free house.

1850 -	Thomas Barnard	1946 - 1951	Joseph Henry Jones
1858 -	William Cooper	1951 - 1955	Alice Lillian Jones
1851 - 1868	James Rushbrook	1956 - 1965	Cyril James Evans
1869 - 1869	Mrs Elizabeth Rushbrook	1966 - 1971	John Paul Shepardson
1870 - 1892	Alfred Smith	1971 - 1974	Guy Dockerill
1893 - 1924	Thomas William Oakey	1975 - 1980	Norman Brown
1924 - 1927	Albert Edward Oakey	1981 - 1982	Serena Yvonne Brown
1928 - 1928	Harry Arthur Croot	1983 - 1985	Michael Anthony Dolphin
1928 - 1940	Joseph Henry Jones	1986 - 1995	Thomas Rainly
1940 - 1945	Alice Lillian Jones	1996 - Curr.	John Borland

GEORGE AND DRAGON

The George and Dragon is believed to originally have stood in Chapel Street, then called Kate's Lane, and occupied the building behind the parked car in the picture, and is shown on Bidwells map of 1851.

The first record of the George & Dragon is in 1820, when the annual licensing session granted a full alehouse license to Joseph Sayer who also was a cooper by trade. On 7th March 1832 Thomas Nash bought "*All that piece of garden ground being in Ely abutting against Kate's Lane and fronting the Turnpike Road leading from Ely to Lynn in breadth upon the front twenty feet and at the lower end seventeen feet*" for £60.

A new building was constructed on the corner of Chapel Street and Lynn Road between 1851 and 1852, as in 1852, Nash & Co put it up for auction and listed it as Lot 27 "*New-built Brick and Slate HOUSE, with YARD behind, and RANGE of BUILDINGS, in Chapel Street, comprising of Cooperage, Stable, Granary, and good Pump of Water.*" and " *This Property is newly built, well situated, and most respectably tenanted*". Ebenezer W Harlock, Ely brewer, purchased the George & Dragon for 395 guineas. This was the building that most people remember the George and Dragon as, number 13, Lynn Road.

In 1888 Bensons advertised a carriers service from the George and Dragon to Southery on Mondays and Thursdays whilst William Washington served Littleport with a daily service, by 1900 Taylors were advertising a service to Prickwillow on Thursdays.

The 1906 Return of Licensed Houses lists it as providing 2 bedrooms for the licensee and 2 bedrooms for lodgers with stabling for 8 horses.

The George and Dragon in the 1950's.

In 1964, the then owners, Steward & Patteson, redecorated the George & Dragon and the sign was taken down and replaced with a temporary one. After 10 years and an article in a local newspaper about the missing sign, the new owners, Watney Mann, hastily hung a new one returning the pub to its full glory.

Right up until its closure customers were treated to "waiter" service from the landlord as there was no bar, just a lounge and Tap-room where ale was tapped direct from the cask in the time honoured tradition.

The property was closed by Watney Mann in June 1978 and later demolished. The plot is today, left vacant due to highway restrictions.

1820 - 1860 Joseph Sayer
1861 - 1864 Hannah Sayer
1865 - 1872 Daniel Holmes
1873 - 1874 Albert Cosyn Allen
1875 - 1878 William Hill
1879 - 1887 Charles William Boon
1888 - 1896 John Mapson
1897 - 1903 John Nicholas
1904 - 1907 Mrs Susan Jeffrey

1908 - 1915 George Vale
1916 - 1921 Edward George Parker
1922 - 1927 George Mickleborough
1928 - 1929 Hannah Elizabeth
              Mickleborough
1930 - 1931 Cyril Watson
1932 - 1954 Leslie Joseph Tingey
1955 - 1958 Stanley Roy Dewey
1958 - 1978 Edward Moden

GLAZIERS' ARMS

The Glaziers' Arms in the 1960's and the vacant plot in 2007

Another of Ely's lost Inns, the Glaziers' Arms, once stood on the eastern corner of Broad Street and Fore Hill. The earliest reference to the "Glaziers" is in 1839 when Greenhill Thomas Day was issued a beer house license. Greenhill Day was a plumber and painter and the pub no doubt was named in recognition of the arms of the trade that Greenhill Day used. On 30th August 1842 the Weights & Measures Inspector charged Greenhill Day with "*short & deficient measures*". In 1856 he was before the magistrates and was charged with "*having his house open for the sale of beer on Sunday 19th October 1856, before half past twelve*" and fined 20s and 10s costs. When Greenhill Day gave up the business, he passed it on to his son in law, Moses Macer, who was a shoemaker from Coveney. At the annual licensing session on 9th September 1869, Moses Macer's application was refused "*due to insufficient ratings*", however his application for 1870 was granted, whether he continued to trade between these times is unclear.

During Perry Piggot Day's tenure, two applications were made to change the license, firstly in 1879, when an application for a spirit license was made, which was refused, and again in 1880, this time an application for a full ale-house license was made, this too was refused. However, during Sarah Day's tenancy, in 1898, the Glaziers Arms gained a full alehouse license, thus allowing it to serve beers, wines and spirits for the first time.

In 1906 Isaac Murfitt, who was also a tailor, ran the pub, which provided the landlord with the use of 1 bedroom and 3 for the use of lodgers, though no stabling was provided.

The Glaziers' Arms was owned by the Day family and leased to Salt & Co of Burton-on-Trent until 1935, when Hall, Cutlack & Harlock, purchased it. On 2nd February 1969 the Glaziers' was closed under Watney Mann's rationalisation programme but the license wasn't surrendered until November 1971. Although the building was demolished, part of the Glaziers' Arms still survives, the sign, which now hangs in the Maltings.

1839 - 1866 Greenhill Thomas Day
1867 - 1869 Moses Macer
1870 - 1875 Moses Macer
1876 - 1892 Perry Piggot Day
1892 - 1900 Mrs Sarah Day
1900 - 1905 Robert J Nicolson
1906 - 1911 Isaac Murfitt
1912 - 1915 Harry Hovell
1915 - 1918 Emily Hovell
1919 - 1926 Harry Hovell
1927 - 1928 Harold Fredrick Scarfe
1929 -   William George Tyrell
1932 - 1933 Walter William Money
1933 - 1941 Frank Bush
1941 - 1945 Mrs Elizabeth Bush
1946 - 1949 Frank Bush
1950 - 1954 Mrs Elizabeth Bush
1955 - 1960 Ronald Seymour
1960 - 1971 William John Pearson

GLOBE

The former Globe beer house, 2007.

On the west side of Broad Street virtually opposite the Railway Inn was the Globe beer house, the building is now an Indian Restaurant. The Globe occupied the right hand side of the current property and is shown on Bidwell's map of 1851 and mentioned in the Valuation list of the same year. After closure the two properties were made into one and a new facade was constructed.

According to the census of 1851, Henry Rickwood was a journeyman and it is highly likely that he named his house after his exploits. An article in the Cambridge Chronicle of June 1855 reported *"Henry Rickwood, beer house keeper was charged by the Supt. Of Police with having his house open for the sale of beer, before half-past twelve in the afternoon, Sunday 24th June. There being a doubt in the case. Dismissed with caution. The defendant was also charged with obstructing and assaulting P.C. Millington whilst in the execution of his duty on Sunday 24th June. Mr Cross, solicitor, was employed by the defendant in both cases, but admitted his client had acted improperly in obstructing the Police Constable. Fined 40s Costs 11s in default, six weeks imprisonment: paid".*

The name the "Globe" is known to have been used at two other sites in Broad Street but when this was is uncertain.

1851 - 1855   Henry Rickwood

GREEN MAN

An illustration of 1882, showing the property that was the one time Green Man, on the corner of the Gallery and Silver St.

One of the oldest of Ely's Inns was the Green Man, formally the Swann, which stood on the corner of the Gallery and Silver Street, formerly called Walpole Lane.

According to the Commonwealth Survey of 1649 the site was described as "*All that messuage or tenement anciently called The Swann in Ely sometime in the tenure of John Stockett and now in the occupation of William Hitch, Clerk....* ". During the time Mr Hitch was at the Inn, he was a Minor Canon of Ely, and had been for some 32 years. It was he, whom Oliver Cromwell had hauled down from the altar, telling him to "*leave off your fooling, and come down, sir*".

The earliest mention of the Green Man is in the Burial Register of St Mary's Ely, where it shows Susan Gregory, Widow, of the Green Man. 8th March 1769. The former Green Man was put up for auction on 18th August 1801 and in the Cambridge Chronicle an advertisement detailed the premises as " *A MESSAUGE or TENEMENT, at the corner of Walpole Lane, next the Gallery, in Ely afore said, late a Public-House, and called the GREEN MAN, together with the Outbuildings, Yard, and large Garden thereto belonging; and TWO TENEMENTS, in Walpole Lane aforesaid, adjoining the same, in the occupation of Mrs. Green and Mr. Thomas Whitechurch*".

In 1858 Rev Harvey Goodwin the Dean of Ely wrote "*The Green man if I rightly remember had all the appearance of being a very ancient hostelry and of having known better days. I could fancy that it was the descendent and representative of a lodging house of the middle ages which had received pilgrims to the shrine of St Etheldreda*".

The Building formally known as the Green Man was demolished in 1880 to make way for what is now part of the Kings School.

1769 -   Susan Gregory   1788 - 1799 Mrs Ann Gambol

HAMMER AND TROWEL

The former Hammer and Trowel in 2007

Situated on the corner of Victoria Street and Annesdale was the Hammer and Trowel beer house which is shown on Bidwell's map of 1851. Opened in 1850, its landlord, a bricklayer, named his premises after the tools of his trade. On 24th October 1853 James Cooper was charged with offences under the "Weights & Measures Act". Mr Cooper's successor was also charged with similar offences, when on the 25th September 1859 at the Weights & Measures sessions "*Mark Benton, beer house keeper Ely*" was charged with "*1 count of having deficient measure*" for which he was fined 5s and 12s 6d costs. Mr Benton was before the courts again when he was charged that on "*18th January 1869 at 3.30, Mark Benton beer retailer, Ely, having his house open before 5 on Sunday*" for this he was fined 40/- and 12/6 costs. Obviously his past conduct had caught up with him, because at the Annual licensing meeting on 25th August 1869 the recently passed "Wine and Beer Act" came into force and Mark Benton of the Red, White and Blue was refused a license on the grounds of "*keeping a house of disorderly character*". Although it was known as the Hammer and Trowel it is believed to have changed its name to the Red, White and Blue in an attempt to gain landlord Benton a new license after his breach of the law earlier in 1869. As a consequence of this refusal it is believed to have closed and today the property exists as a private residence.

1850 - 1855 James Cooper   1858 - 1869 Mark Benton

HEREWARD

The Hereward has the distinction of being Ely's newest pub, situated in Market Street, opposite the Town House pub. The Barracuda Group, occupying the premises that were formally the Cutlack family's Ironmongers business, opened it in May 2005.

2005 - Current   Anthony Love

HIGH FLYER

The High Flyer is situated in Newnham Street and takes its name from a horse bred in Bury St Edmunds. As a three year old he won 800 guineas in a sweepstake and before being sold in 1779, to Richard Tattersall for £2,500, had won eight races. Mr Tattersall, while living at High Flyer Hall entertained the then Prince of Wales, later George IV and his friends. On 18th October1793, at the age of nineteen, High Flyer died. A day of national mourning was kept and subsequently several ships were named after him.

During the mid to late 1800s the High Flyer was occasionally known as the Black Horse

On 23rd August 1848 at the annual licensing meeting, Daniel Cuttriss had his license suspended for a week, along with his other brothers, to "*allow the magistrates time to consider the most desirable steps to be taken to stop the torrent of vice and infamy consequent upon the irregular and improper manner in which he conducted his house*", and on 28th December 1850 he was summoned before the magistrates for "*allowing drunkenness and other disorderly conduct in his house*". He was again back in front of the magistrates for having "*his house open for the sale of beer before half past twelve on Sunday 19th October 1856.*

The case was proved and the defendant being an old offender was fined 40s with costs".

It was listed in the 1906 Returns of Licensed Houses as having 3 bedrooms for the licensee and 1 for lodgers with stabling for 12 horses and 3 vehicles. When the Ely Horticultural Society was formed after the First World War it was based at the High Flyer public house and during the 1920's and 30's it helped raise funds for Addenbrooke's Hospital in Cambridge. It also ran a fishing club, even though it was some distance from the river, from the mid 1900's up until 1982. A popular Slate Club was run for its regulars.

The High Flyer in the 1960's advertising Ely Ales.

The "Flyer" carried a full alehouse license and was owned by Henry Hall in 1875, it remained a Hall house up to the mergers of the mid 1900's when it become a Watney Mann house in 1969 and currently the pub is owned by Punch Taverns Plc. It was extended and refurbished in the early 1990's and is still open today offering a restaurant and provision of 6 bedrooms for lodging customers.

1790 - 1811 William Dench
1812 - 1814 Samuel Shearman
1815 - 1817 John Shelton
1818 - 1834 Martin Hodson
1835 - 1840 Sarah Hodson
1841 - 1845 Thomas Marsh
1846 - 1872 Daniel Cuttriss
1873 - 1900 John Mansfield Knowles
1901 - 1908 George Knowles
1908 - 1922 William Arthur Dougall
1923 - 1927 Walter Bex
1928 - 1936 George Taylor
1937 - 1941 Mrs Mildred Harriet Taylor
1942 - 1942 Mrs Fox
1942 - 1944 Fredrick Hall
1945 - 1950 Albert Edward Well
1950 - 1956 William Henry Stopp
1957 - 1968 William Edward Collen
1969 - 1970 Cyril Wilfred Stevens
1971 - 1974 Fredrick Joseph Harris
1974 - 1992 Albert Victor Hearn
1992 - 1993 Colin James Murfitt
1994 - 1996 M.Niadoo
1996 - 1999 David Alistair Peters
2000 - 2000 Janet Watson
2001 - 2002 Graham Sharp
2003 - 2003 Jason Clifford Pearce
2004 -   Sharon Ansell
2006 - Curr. Krysia Wasowski

JOLLY FARMERS

The former Jolly Farmers as it is in 2007

Situated on the west end of Railway Terrace at what is now number 3, Castlehythe was the Jolly Farmers, licensed as a beer house. This pub had a relatively short life, the earliest reference to it is in 1850 and the closure dated is unknown. Landlord, Thomas Hudson was also a Blacksmith by trade.

1850 -1854 Thomas Hudson

KING CHARLES IN THE OAK

The King Charles in the Oak on the corner of Station Road circa 1910.

The King Charles in the Oak stood on the corner of Station Road and Annesdale, often referred to as the Royal Oak or Oak in the mid 1800s, it had various owners including Augustus Ekin and P L Hudson, brewer, of Pampisford until it was sold to Hall, Cutlack & Harlock on 20th July 1942.

Landlord John Seymour was before the Magistrates on 21st July 1849 when he was charged with "*keeping his house open at unauthorized hours*". The Cambridge Chronicle reported a tragic incident that occurred on 15th August 1851 "*The Grandchild (6 years of age) of Mr Seymoor, landlord of the Oak Public house near the Station was missing and could not be found anywhere. The child's friends became alarmed and a search was made in every direction without gaining the least clue. The police rendered all possible assistance in their power. Early the following morning, she was discovered by Mr Gotobed, a neighbour, drowned in a small catch-water drain opposite the Angel Inn and not more than 50 yards from her home. Verdict: found drowned, fell in whilst collecting flowers*".

John Seymour was charged on the 23rd September 1859 with having 4 counts of "*deficient measures*", he was fined 7s 6d and 12s 6d costs and on 27th May 1885 William King was charged with "*allowing gaming for beer with dominoes*", though the charge was later dropped.

Licensed as a beer house throughout its life, the pub offered 4 bedrooms to lodgers and travellers with stabling for 2 horses.

Mr J Tunnel was in court for non-payment of income tax, £1/19/4d on 3rd June 1948, however, after the King Charles closed on the 5th April 1949, he bought the building from the brewery as there is reference in court registers to "*J Tunnel taking possession of 23, Station Road*" on 3rd November 1949.

The site of the former King Charles in 2007.

1847 - 1867 John Seymour
1869 - 1881 Joseph Sorrell
1881 - 1884 Richard Palmer
1885 - 1894 William King
1895 - 1898 Mark Benton
1899 - 1900 James Royston
1900 - 1901 H C Gerischer
1902 - 1908 Fredrick James Pluck

1908 - 1909 Walter Thompson
1910 - 1924 John Webb
1925 - 1929 Ernest Sydney Longley
1930 - 1933 George James King
1934 - 1936 Fredrick Arthur Clarke
1937 - 1938 Mr Gay
1938 - 1939 Mr Aston
1940 - 1949 J Tunnell

KING WILLIAM IV

Number 29, Lynn Road, on the corner with Egremont Street, is the former King William IV public house. It opened when the 1830 Beer House Act was passed and held a beer house license through out its history, although applications for an alehouse were made in 1860 and 1880 but these were refused.

On 19th June 1830 Robert Barber mortgaged a property from Elizabeth Seymour for £180, described as *"All that messuage or tenement situated, standing and being in Ely fronting the Turnpike Road leading from Ely to Littleport towards the East; Acremen Street North; a piece of garden ground belonging to Jon Walker West; and the premises of David Ellingham South"*. Then on 28th January 1841 Robert Barber mortgaged the property to William Cutlack, of Littleport, Common Brewer.

In an auction notice for 30th June 1842 the King William 4th was described as *"All that Capital Freehold, and well accustomed Public-House, situate In St Mary's Parish, Ely, opposite the Shire Hall, called or known by the name or sign of William The Fourth containing three large rooms and a Cellar on the ground floor, also three spacious Sleeping-Rooms, together with a large Yard adjoining the same and convenient Stable and outbuildings"*.

As well as running the pub, John Allen was also a baker and Daniel Elvish would have run an orderly house, as he was a Police pensioner.

In 1900 Russels advertised a Carriers service from the "King Billy" to Littleport on Thursdays.

The 1906 Returns of Licensed Houses shows the "King Billy" as having 1 bedroom for the licensee's family and 2 for lodgers with stabling for 6 horses and 2 vehicles.

The King William IV shortly after closure.

William Cutlack was shown as the owner in 1841 and held the house until merging with Harlock's brewery in 1908. On 29th August 1962 Steward & Patterson closed the King William and the property is now a private residence.

1830 - 1841	Robert Barber	1899 - 1900	Walter Thompson
1847 - 1851	Mrs Catherine Barber	1901 - 1907	Daniel Elvish
1858 - 1873	John Payne Allen	1908 - 1916	Mrs Susannah Elvish
1874 - 1877	Thomas Dann	1917 - 1952	Fred Oakey
1878 - 1879	William James Topping	1952 - 1960	Samuel Giddens
1879 - 1898	William Evans	1961 - 1962	Horace Jones

KING'S ARMS

The King's Arms is situated in St Mary's Street and held a full alehouse license. In the Cambridge Chronicle of the 5th September 1807, the King's Arms was advertised for auction and described as *"Substantial messuage with adjoining tenement, spacious yard, excellent garden well stocked, convenient outbuildings and stabling for 20 horses"*.

In 1823, carriers were leaving the King's Arms for London on Monday, Wednesday and Friday afternoons, Downham on Tuesdays, Thursdays and Saturdays and Sutton on Thursdays and Saturdays.

In 1826 Henry Salmon, Butcher of Ely, was found guilty of having assaulted Samuel Myrton, innkeeper, on 6th February that year. Mr Myrton had previously been assaulted by Mr Salmon and did not consider himself secure from his violence in future. Salmon was sentenced to 1 month in prison in Ely and *"be further imprisonment until he should give surety to keep the peace himself a £20 and 2 sureties in £10 each"*. A tragic accident occurred in April 1828 when *"a child (about 3 years old) of Mr Myrton, of the King's Arms, fell into a cistern in the yard and drowned. The lad not missing for more than 5 minutes, but with every effort to restore animation was without effect"*. The Coroner's verdict was accidental death.

In 1840 Thurborn, carriers, were leaving for Sutton every Thursday, with Elger's to Haddenham whilst between 1850 and 1864 Nunns, carriers, advertised a service to Sutton on Thursdays.

When the Mounted Rifle Corps was established in 1860, a ceremony was held at the Kings Arms on the 25th June to celebrate its inauguration. The members, under leadership of Moses Oates, Esquire, Captain, included men from Coveney, Sutton, Wilburton, Haddenham, Witchford and Ely.

Between 1869 and 1879, Bells the Carriers advertised a service to Mepal and Chatteris.

The King's Arms circa 1910.

In 1875 Eyre & Co, brewers, of Kings Lynn were shown as the owner and supplier to the King's Arms but by 1884 it had passed to Henry Hall, brewer of Ely. It remained a Hall's house until the mergers of the mid 1900's. Today it is owned by Enterprise Inns Plc.

The King's Arms was listed in 1906 as having 5 bedrooms for the licensee's use and 1 for lodgers with stabling for 9 horses and 24 vehicles.

John Titterton, (1830-1914) both artist and local historian writes *"The last reputed witch burnt at Ely came out of a house upon the site of which the King's Arms is built"*.

1790 - 1796 Luke Dench	1921 - 1931 Herbert John Gregory
1797 - 1801 William Freeman	1932 - 1957 Hector Macdonald Parrington Wenn
1802 - 1807 Ann Freeman	
1808 - 1808 James Reynlods	1957 - 1959 Fredrick George Curtis
1809 - 1815 James Howse	1959 - 1960 Graham Arthur Charles Fisher
1816 - 1818 Samuel Myrton	
1819 - 1819 James Shaw	1961 - 1973 Samuel Giddons
1820 - 1844 Samuel Myrton	1974 - 1976 Michel Honore Dasseville
1845 - 1847 Sarah Myrton	1976 - 1977 Robert Alfred Leslie Plane
1848 - 1862 Edward Luddington	1978 - 1980 Brian John Smith
1863 - 1869 Robert Joselyn	1981 - 1985 Michael Richard Swain
1870 - 1878 James Norman	1985 - 1993 Brian Butler
1879 - 1897 John Bell	1994 - 1997 John Edward White
1898 - 1898 Francis Bell	1998 - 1998 Ann Fuller
1899 - 1900 Fredrick John Cook	1999 - 2004 Graham Young
1901 - 1917 Nathan Robinson	2007 - Curr. Andrew James King
1918 - 1920 Charles James Gregory	

LAMB INN

The Lamb occupies a prominent position at the junction of Lynn Road and St Mary's Street with High Street and the Gallery. It dates back to the time of King Richard II. In 1416 Bishop Fordham mentions the inn in a survey he made of all his properties in Ely. At this time Julian Barbour was the occupant though it cannot be said if the inn was named the Lamb at this time though it is probable, for the lamb was one of the signs to be adopted by medieval innkeepers. Standing close to the Cathedral and monastery buildings it would be most likely to be known by the sign of the *Agnus Dei*, the Lamb of God. It was certainly called the Lamb in 1672 as John Cuthbert, tenant of the Manor of Ely Barton, died and his son was admitted to a messuage next to "*le howse called the Holy Lambe*", it is again mentioned in 1667 when the Feoffees of Parsons' Charity "*expended at the Lambe 3s 0d*".

It was not until the 18th century, with the formation of the Turnpike roads, that the Lamb came to dominate the main approaches to Ely. It was a meeting place for the Turnpike Trustees and also for St. Mary's churchwardens who occasionally held their dinner at the Lamb, the expenditure on liquid refreshment often exceeding that of the food. During this time the inn was also noted for cock fighting, having its own cockpit.

The Lamb Inn 1908.

In 1732 the Lamb, owned by Mary Outlaw of Haddenham, was sold to Thomas Tingey for £160, he had held the Lamb on lease for the previous 12 months but now purchased the property, paying a yearly rent of one peppercorn. In 1782 Henry Corney was the tenant landlord as Sarah Granger, widow of the late Thomas Granger, sold the Lamb to William Harlock, common brewer, of Ely. It consisted of "*a messuage, tenement or inn called and known by the sign of the Lamb, with maltings, malt mill, malt kiln, brewhouse, stable, outhouses, yards, gardens, ways, waters and water-courses*".

John Harlock leased the inn to William Reynolds who entered in to an agreement to "*take all ale and beer used in the inn from John Harlock*". Thus ending the brewing of beer on this site. The agreement also provided that "*the house used as a mill house shall be converted in to a coach house and the store house and brew house be converted into stables*", from this its evident that the coaching trade was of great importance at this time.

In 1823 the "Union" ran from Lynn to Cambridge on Mondays, Wednesdays and Fridays departing at 11.00 from the Lamb. The "Telegraph" ran from Upwell to Cambridge on Tuesdays, Thursdays and Saturdays.

The original building was a much smaller, less grand affair but with the increase in coaching traffic a new building was erected on the site making the Lamb the most prominent posting house in the city for the long distance coaches for in 1828 William and John Harlock advertised the inn for let and William Beecroft, innkeeper, of the White Hart moved to the Lamb. An advert of 1st July 1828 stated that "*William Beecroft, ... begs to state that the Lamb Inn being about to be rebuilt upon an extensive scale and with every regard to the convenience and comfort of the public he has engaged a commodious house near the inn, where he proposes to carry on the business during the erection of the new buildings. Posting with good horses and steady Drivers"*. In 1829 an advert in the Cambridge Chronicle stated that Wm Beecroft had moved to *"a spacious house and premises lately erected on the site of the old Lamb Inn"*. This is the inn that is still in use today. When William Beecroft was retiring from business, the Lamb was advertised on February 1843, to be let by auction as *"Family Hotel and Posting-house, called the Lamb at Ely, comprising handsome Entrance, well situated Bar, Commercial Room, Market Room, Large Dining Room, and Four other excellent sitting rooms, and capable of making up twenty beds, large and convenient Kitchen and extensive Cellerage. The Yard is spacious, and contains two lock-up Coach-houses, Capital Stabling for Thirty horses, suitable and well arranged Offices with Convenient Tap, fronting Market Street"*. *"The Tenant is restricted only to Malt Liquor"*.

In 1845 the first railway reached Ely and the Lamb was more than able to meet the demands of the new era, which spelt the start of the demise of the coaching days. A lady who had arrived in Ely by rail in 1894 found the City *"diminutive and sleepy"*. She was also struck by the food offered at a Lucretian feast at the Lamb, where she dined on roast lamb, asparagus, strawberries and cream and Cottenham cheeses, she remarked *"It is possible to dine both unwisely and exceeding well"*. During the late 1800s an omnibus was advertised to and from the station to meet every train.

In 1906 the Lamb was listed as having 5 bedrooms for the landlords use and 15 for lodgers with stabling for 15 horses and 12 vehicles. By comparison it now boasts 31 bedrooms. During the mid 1980s the old coaching stables were converted in to a new venue called the Fenman Bar, which closed shortly after 2000, and is now used as a function room.

After William Harlock bought the inn in 1782 it remained in the Harlock family until 1950 when East Anglian Breweries was formed, it passed through various owners including Steward & Patteson, Watney Mann, Old English Inns PLC and is now in the hands of Greene King who bought it in September 2001. Originally licensed as an alehouse, the Lamb is the last of Ely's old coaching inns and still caters for tourists and the travelling public, though today the motorcar has replaced the horse and carriage.

1416 - Julian Barbour	1951 - 1952 Catherine Esme May
1690 - 1714 Thomas Kempton	1952 - 1953 Fredrick George Hards
1719 - Henry Kempton	1954 - 1954 William John Milne
1731 - 1762 Thomas Tingey	1954 - 1956 Fredrick George Hards
1763 - 1776 Thomas Pratt	1956 - 1963 Brian Walsh Howarth
1777 - 1782 Henry Corney	1963 - 1963 Victor Toni
1782 - William Reynolds	1963 - 1966 Wesley Callard
1790 - 1808 Robert Genn	1966 - 1968 Ian Dawson James
1809 - 1825 Henry Rance	1969 - 1970 Thomas Fletcher Algernon Burt
1826 - 1827 Martha Rance	
1828 - 1843 William Beecroft	1970 - 1970 Norman Goode
1843 - 1857 Hugh Boughen	1971 - 1971 Miss Rita Joan Baldwin

1858 - 1872 Susannah Paris Waller	1972 - 1972 Roger Patrick Chambers
1873 - 1873 Lucy Maria Stansall	1973 - 1974 Christopher John Fancourt
1874 - 1879 Jesse Batcheler	1974 - 1974 Alexander Edgar Grant
1880 - 1881 Henry Wilson Ellis	1975 - 1975 Mary Francis Barry
1882 - 1895 James French	1975 - 1979 Terence John Hunter Brown
1896 - 1903 Frank Moyes	
1904 - 1920 Sydney Airey	1979 - 1981 Richard William Scoble
1921 - 1929 Kelsick Inman	1982 - 1982 David Howard White
1929 - 1932 Capt. William Geo Rivers	1983 - 1994 Gerald James Bell
1932 - 1937 George Andrew Martin	1995 - 1995 Ian Hugh Tiggy
1937 - 1942 Geoffrey Littlejohn Ogilvy	1995 - 1998 Robert Lilley
1943 - 1946 Oscar Borer	1998 - 1999 Edward Olzak
1946 - 1947 Thomas Edwin Langton	1999 - 2003 Paul Leitch
1948 - 1951 Fredrick George Hards	2007 - Curr. Alan Sillett

LAMB TAP

The former Lamb Tap in 2007.

In common with most Inns, the Lamb had a bar for the "working classes" to enjoy refreshments; this was called the "Lamb Tap". It was situated at the Market Street entrance to the Inn.

1866 - 1871 Thomas Cropely	1908 - T Underhill
1893 - John Boone	1912 - Sydney Airey
- 1900 Jonathan Mapson	1920 - Mrs Clarke
1902 - Henry Rosbrook	1956 - Timothy Allman

MAID'S HEAD

At number 51, Fore Hill, nearly opposite the Anchor, once stood the Maid's Head. The property occupied a plot that had an entrance onto Bull Lane (Lisle Lane) nearly opposite Willow Walk.

In the 1852 auction of Nash & Co of Royston, Lot 32 was the Maid's Head, and was described as " *A Brick and Tile HOUSE, containing Tap Room, Front and Back Parlours, Cellar, Kitchen, Dairy, and Four Bed Rooms, large Yard, Pump, Stables, Lodges, and Back Entrance into Bull Lane*". Marshalls of Huntingdon bought the Maid's Head for 370 guineas.

In 1908 the pub was listed as having 4 bedrooms for the licensee's family and 2 for lodgers, with stabling for 4 horses. In 1932, Marshall's became part of Huntingdon Breweries Ltd, five years later the Maid's Head closed.

On the 3rd February 1937, the Spirit retailers (ordinary, ale-house) license was transferred to the Rifleman's Arms. The building has since been demolished and new housing stands on the site.

1790 - 1804 Butler Cole	1872 - 1874 Ruben Hunt
1805 - 1833 Sarah Cole	1875 - 1878 Elijah Smith
1834 - 1835 John Balls	1879 - 1899 James Roberts
1836 - 1837 William Bradley	1900 - 1900 Sarah Ann Roberts
1837 - 1871 Robert Wade	1901 - 1937 Robert Lupson

MALT AND HOPS

The Former Malt and Hops public house as it is in 2007.

Number 4, Church Lane was once the Malt and Hops public house. As the name suggests, there was a brewery on the premises though no date for this is available. Ely brewer, Thomas Legge, owned and supplied the pub in 1851

On 22nd August 1861 James Gross made an application for a full (Alehouse) license but this was refused.

In 1908 the pub was listed as having 2 Bedrooms for the landlord's use and 3 for lodgers, but no stabling was available.

The Malt and Hops was licensed as a beer house up to its closure, by East Anglian Breweries on the 1 February 1956. Today the property is a private residence.

1850 - 1851 Charles Searle	1902 - 1923 Robert James Sindall
1858 - 1877 James Gross	1924 - 1933 Jonathan Wilson
1878 - 1882 Sarah Gross	1934 - 1946 George Herbert Bailey
1883 - 1895 William John Richmond	1946 - 1950 F Vickers
1896 - 1901 Alfred Barton	1950 - 1956 Cyril James Evans

MARQUIS OF GRANBY

The Marquis of Granby displaying a painted advert for Ely Ales and Stouts sometime after its closure and the property as it is in 2007.

On the South side of Victoria Street is number 6, formerly the Marquis of Granby. Named after General John Manners, son of the Duke of Rutland, he was a noble soldier who was popular with his men, and for his favoured soldiers, he often provided funds for them to purchase public houses on their retirement.

It is believed that Victoria Street was built around 1850 so it is likely that the Marquis opened about 1851. Landlord James Cuttriss, who was also a Whitesmith by trade, was charged with an offence "*under Alehouse Act*" on 9th February 1852 which may have led to him selling his house as an advert in the Cambridge Chronicle on 15th May 1852 stated " *for sale, a freehold Public house situate in Victoria Street Ely, leading to the Railway Station known as The Marquis of Granby with two newly erected Dwelling houses adjoining*".

Ruth Lister fell foul of the weights and measures inspector when she was charged on 23rd September 1859 for 3 counts of having deficient measures, she was fined 10s and 12.6d costs.

The Marquis ran one of the fishing clubs that was popular with anglers from the Midlands in the early 1900's, and had 2 Bedrooms for the lodgers though no stabling was available. It also ran a Slate Club for its regulars in the mid 1900's.

Licensed as a beer house, the Marquis was owned and supplied by Eyres brewery of Kings Lynn from 1874 to 1904, when Morgan's brewery of Norwich took over Eyres brewery and subsequently the Marquis, until its closure in 1939.

1851 James Cuttriss	1915 - 1920 Alfred George Talbot
1855 - 1859 Mrs Ruth Lister	1921 - 1921 Alfred William Robinson
1864 - William Howe	1922 - 1929 Arthur William Sawyer
1869 - 1878 John Stute	1929 - 1929 William George Tyrell
1879 - 1881 Mrs Martha Stute	1929 - Walter William Money
1881 - 1881 George Feetham	1933 - 1935 James Robert Burton
1882 - 1900 Mrs Fanny Richardson	1935 - 1937 Sydney Reginald Taylor
1900 - 1914 Ernest William Wilson	1938 - 1939 William Barrett

MINSTER

The Minster Tavern in 2007.

Standing close to the Cathedral on Minster Place is the Minster Tavern. Originally known as the Greyhound, it first held a full alehouse licence in 1817 and was owned by the Hills family.

An advertisement appeared in the Cambridge Chronicle of 6th October 1817 describing John Hills new business *"London Porter and Spirituous Liquors, John Hills, Porter and Spirituous Liquor Merchant, fronting the High Street, Ely, informs his friends and the Public in general that he will be on SATURDAY next, the 11th instant, commence BUSINESS in the above lines; and he has laid in a STOCK of LIQUORS of the first quality from eminent houses in LONDON: and of the best LONDON PORTER, Draught and Bottled, from the House of Barclay & Co, and he begs to assure those who may honour him with their commands, that the utmost attention shall be paid to the execution of their orders, and the business conducted on the most reasonable terms"*.

In 1906 it was listed as having 5 bedrooms but unusually there were none for lodgers and no stabling was available. By 1915 Henry J Jones had become the owner.

In 1944 it changed its name to the Minster Wine Vaults and another change in 1976 saw it become what we know today as the Minster Tavern. It remained a free house until George Daters sold it to Bass-Charrington in 1983. Today it is owned by Mitchell & Butler who are a trading arm of Bass-Charrington.

1817 - 1835 John Hills	1944 - 1963 George Maurice Barker
1836 - 1838 Elizabeth Hills	1964 - 1971 Charles Arthur Hewitt
1839 - 1885 John Hills	1971 - 1974 Ian Russell Pugh
1886 - 1889 Elizabeth Hills	1975 - 1976 Ian Duncan Wilkinson
1889 - 1913 Charles Hills	1977 - 1978 Peter William Foster
1914 - 1914 Lucy Vincent Hills	1979 - 1983 George Earnest Stanley Daters
1915 - 1916 Stokely Hutchinson Fisher	
1917 - 1918 Ernest William Wilson	1984 - 1989 Anthony Mervyn Howard-Tripp
- 1922 Henry Julius Jones	
1923 - 1931 Edwin John Price	1990 - 2002 Dennis Sharp
1931 - 1932 Margaret Grace Price	2002 - 2003 Ian Robinson
1933 - 1934 John Brown	2004 - 2006 Nicholas Hugh Collingwood
1934 - 1938 John Scarfe	2006 - Curr. David Wall
1938 - 1943 John Leopold Hunter	

NEW INN

Situated on Lynn Road on the site now occupied by the Paddocks housing development was the New Inn. The Inn is shown on Bidwell's map of 1851 as detached and standing back from the road. It was owned and supplied by Thomas Legge, brewer, of Ely. No mention of the Inn appears after 1851.

1839 - 1847 William Benstead   1850 - 1851 John Hall

ODD FELLOWS ARMS

Situated on the corner of New Barns Road and Bohemond Street was the Odd Fellows Arms. The building still exists as a private residence.

The Odd Fellows Arms takes its name from the mutual friendly society of the same name, and is unlikely to have existed before 1850, as these organizations were illegal up until that date. Mention is made of a Beer retailer on New Barns Road in 1850 and the Pub is shown on Bidwells map of 1851. William Kempton, who was also a cabinet-maker, made an application for a full (alehouse) license on 27th August 1851 but this was refused. He died on 15th March 1854 after that no reference is made of the Odd Fellows Arms.

The former Oddfellows Arms in 2007.

1850 - 1854   William Kempton

PEACOCK

Situated in St Mary's Street was the Peacock Inn. The earliest known date of the Peacock is 1605 when Robert Walden, by will gave a rent-charge of £1 per annum payable out of a house in Ely for the preaching of two sermons annually, and gave another rent-charge of equal amount for the same purposes payable out of a public house in Ely known by the sign of the Peacock. The same fee is referred to again as being charged to " *the house of Jonas Wilkes (known by the sign of the Peacock)*" in a report "*made, as directed by Bishop Yorke at his Primary Visitation, in 1783*".

The Peacock was sold by auction at The Red Lion on 25th May 1814 and described in an advertisement in the Cambridge Chronicle as " *All that well-known accustomed Public-House called the Peacock, desirably situate in the principle street, in Ely St. Mary's afore said, together with an old-established Blacksmith's Shop attached, with good Garden and convenient outbuildings thereto belonging, as the same is now, and has been many years, in the occupation of Mr. JOHN KING, under a lease which expires at Lady-Day, 1817*".

In 1855 George Ellis was "*cautioned as to his future conduct and fined 5s with 11s costs for refusing entry to P.C. Howe and Saunders at 3am on the 23rd February, who were looking for two women of light character with lodgings in the house, suspected of having stolen a gold ring from Robert Griffin*".

The Peacock after its closure and as it is in 2007.

For most of its life the Peacock was also a Blacksmiths and many of the licensees carried on the trade as Blacksmith/Farrier as well as running the Inn. In 1906 it was listed as providing its licensee with 2 bedrooms and 3 for lodgers with stabling for 9 horses and 6 vehicles.

The Peacock was licensed as a full alehouse and was owned from 1875 by Henry Hall and remained in the Hall family until the mid 1900 mergers. It closed on the 3rd March 1955 and the license was transferred to the West End. Today the property, number 32, is used by the Education Authority.

1783 - Jonas Wilkes	1880 - 1881 John Cole
1790 - 1818 John King	1882 - 1890 Thomas Hoult
1819 - 1835 Mary King	1890 - 1892 James Snowling
1836 - 1848 John King	1892 - 1896 Mrs Rebecca Snowling
1849 - 1856 George Ellis	1897 - 1901 George Sewell
1857 - 1861 Robert King	1902 - 1902 No return
1862 - 1873 John Cole	1903 - 1904 Matthew Thompson
1874 - 1874 No return	1905 - 1928 Mrs Rebecca Sewell
1875 - 1876 William Dent	1928 - 1940 George Sewell
1877 - 1879 Charles William Joselyn	1940 - 1955 Mrs Emily Baden Sewell

PLOUGH AND FLEECE

The former Plough and Fleece when it was the Kum in Café during the 1950's and the site in 2007.

Once standing at 43, St Mary's Street opposite the junction with West End and Cambridge Road was the Plough & Fleece. The building was believed to date back to C1725 and was of a timber-framed construction. It was used for the St Mary's workhouse until a new Ely Union workhouse was built further up Cambridge Road (later the Tower Hospital) and was opened in 1837. The property was taken over by Ely brewer F.L.Harlock and around 1850 it became the Plough and Fleece.

Landlord Francis Mayhew was charged under the weights and measures act of having "*3 counts of deficient measures*" on 18th august 1859, he was fined 5s and costs of 12s 6d.

In 1881 William Lavender was fined 12/6 for "*permitting drunkenness at Ely on 7th May*" at noon.

In 1906 it provided its landlord with 3 bedrooms and 1 for lodgers with stabling for 4 horses and 4 vehicles.

The Plough & Fleece held a beer house license and was supplied by Harlock's brewery and Hall, Cutlack & Harlock until the licence was dropped in 1932 and the premises became the " KUM-IN-CAFÉ". Although the property was listed as being of architectural and historical significance, it was demolished in 1962 to make way for new housing and offices.

1850 - 1851 William Smith	1885 - 1896 Mark Runham
1858 - 1864 Francis Mayhew	1897 - 1900 George James Ellis
1866 - 1867 Edward Hamey	1901 - 1910 John Lavender
1869 - 1869 Benjamin Pointer	1911 - 1918 John Dring
1869 - 1884 William Lavender	1919 - 1922 Miss Elizabeth Dring
1884 - 1884 Elizabeth Lavender	1922 - 1930 Albert Leach

PRINCE ALBERT

The Prince Albert stands in Silver Street, an area once closely associated with the Ely Militia, although the pub was not originally where it is today. Bidwell's map of 1851 shows the Prince Albert opposite, where houses numbers 19 - 25 are now, the current buildings being built on its site. It is believed the current "Albert" was built in 1869, as there is a brick with the inscription "J.D. 1869" near an upper window, but when it moved there is unclear.

The first landlord, Michael Dexter was charged on 14th February 1842 with "*keeping house open during divine service*" and in the 1851 census he was listed as "*Sergeant of the Militia on pay*". In 1858 he was before the magistrates on the 7th October charged with "*having his house open for the sale of beer before 12.30pm on Sunday*" for which he was fined 10s with 10s costs, in default of 21 days imprisonment.

John Cooper made applications in 1860, 1861 and 1863 for a full (Alehouse) license but these were refused each time and on the 18th November 1866 he was charged with "*offences under Beer Act, convicted and penalty of 7/6 with 11/6 costs*". The following year he did not reapply for a license.

The Prince Albert during the 1960's and in 2007.

In the 1906 Returns of Licensed Houses, the "Albert" was listed as providing 2 bedrooms for the licensee's use and 4 for lodgers with stabling for one horse. As with most pubs of the time, the Prince Albert ran a Slate Club for its regulars during the War years.

Licensed as a beer house, the Albert was in 1849 owned by William Apthorpe, by 1892 it had passed to Greene King of Bury St Edmunds who still supplies the pub to this day.

1842 - 1858 Michael Dexter	1949 - 1951 George Fredrick Pryke
1860 - 1866 John Cooper	1952 - 1952 Reginald Jack Good
1867 - 1872 John Matthews	1953 - 1953 Florence Elsie Good
1872 - 1872 Mrs Matilda Matthews	1954 - 1957 Fredrick William Tedora
1873 - 1885 Robert Ellingham	1957 - 1959 Archibald Fredrick Orsbourne
1885 - 1889 Mrs Catherine Ellingham	
1889 - 1892 Rbt Mendham Ellingham	1960 - 1964 Alfred Edward Hall
1892 - 1892 Elizabeth Rose Ellingham	1965 - 1968 Reginald Duncan Gawthrop
1893 - 1896 Thomas Denton	1969 - 1969 Victor Thomas James Finn
1897 - 1903 Jonathan Minnett	1970 - 1975 Charles Alfred Newbold
1904 - 1910 John William Smith	1976 - 1981 Reginald Edmund Woodland
1911 - 1922 John Woodbine	
1923 - 1931 Fred Snowling	1982 - 1984 Gary Ernest Briars
1931 - 1942 James William Spencer	1985 - 1989 John Henry Champion
1942 - 1949 John James Gull	1990 - Curr. Ernest Michael Hunt

QUEEN'S HEAD

The Queen's Head on Quayside with the Ship in the distance circa 1900 and as it is in 2007.

Situated on the Waterside at number 54, the Queen's Head had one of the most desirable locations of the time. The building still stands and is now a private residence.

The earliest recorded date for the Queen's Head is 1757 when a *"Title of devisees of the late John Pond to a messuage in Ely being a public house called the Queen's Head, being freehold*' when it was bequeathed to Luke Dench.

When Luke Dench left the Queen's Head, it was put up for auction and in an advertisement in the Cambridge Chronicle dated 12th September 1807 it was described as " *That valuable and well accustomed PUBLIC HOUSE, the Queen's Head, consisting of substantial brick and tile Messuage, with a Granary and Black-smiths shop-adjoining, spacious Yard, convenient outbuildings and good stabling, pleasantly situate within a few yards of the navigable river leading from Lynn to Cambridge, and from its situation is capable of great improvement*'.

Edward Few was in breach of his license as he was charged on the 8th November 1851 with *"keeping open Alehouse on a Sunday"*. He must have conducted an orderly house from then on, as he kept the license until 1862.

Henry Hall became the new owner, until 1897 when it passed to A&B Hall who continued to own and supply the Inn up to its closure.

The 1906 Return of Licensed Houses listed the Queen's Head as providing 1 bedroom for the licensee and 5 for lodgers with stabling for 2 horses and 2 vehicles.

The Queen's Head was licensed throughout as an alehouse and closed in 1913 under the 1904 Licensing Act compensation scheme.

1790 - 1801 Alice Laurence	1850 - 1861 Edward Few
1802 - 1807 Luke Dench	1862 - 1865 William Henry Norman
1808 - 1808 John Thorpe	1866 - 1873 John Fenn
1809 - 1813 Daniel Russell	1874 - 1875 Jeremiah Fenn
1814 - 1831 William Bodger	1876 - 1880 Ann Fenn
1832 - 1836 Frances Bodger	1881 - 1882 John Long Fenn
1837 - 1837 David Patington	1883 - 1892 Nathan Eley
1838 - 1841 Henry Parsons	1893 - 1894 Mary Ann Eley
1842 - 1846 Mrs Frances Parsons	1895 - 1913 William English Hall
1847 - 1849 William Roan	

RAILWAY INN

The Railway Inn was situated on the East side of Broad Street in the centre of what is now the entrance to the Jubilee Gardens. As the railway reached Ely in 1845 it is unlikely to have existed before then, however the earliest reference to the beer house is 1847. Mr Gooby was charged with offences *"under Beer Act, dismissed on payment of 5/-"'* on 29th May 1856, by the following year John Harris held the license. It is presumed to have closed in 1869 when at the Annual Licensing meeting on the 25th August that year the application was *"refused due to keeping a house of disorderly character"* this was a result of the recently passed Beer and Wine act of that year which was to try and reduce the amount of drunkenness and lawlessness that accompanied the massive increase in numbers of beer houses at the time. Mr Harris moved to the Three Blackbirds in 1871.

1847 - 1856 James Gooby   1857 -1869 John Harris

RAILWAY TAVERN

The former Railway Tavern (with double apex frontage) circa 1910 and the site as it is in 2007.

Once standing on Station Road (formally Bridge Road) was the Railway Tavern. Built to capitalise from the new railway, which arrived in the city in 1845. The Railway Tavern held a beer house license, with Lindsells, brewers, of Chatteris owning and supplying the Inn. Walter Womack had not been landlord for long when he was charged on the 15th June 1851 with " *Disorderly conduct in keeping his house open* " he later made an application for a full alehouse license on the 25th August 1852, which was refused, however his application of the 14th May 1853 was granted even though it was opposed by Mr Harlock and Mr Hall !

On 23rd June 1855 Mr Womack, who was an "old offender" was charged for "*having his house open for the sale of beer after 10pm on Sunday 24th June, the Superintendent of Police having seen one person leave the house at 11.20pm with three quarts of beer, and shortly afterwards another person left with a quantity in a jug, He was fined 40s with costs of 11s and cautioned as to his future conduct*".

In 1906 the Inn was shown to provide its landlord with 1 bedroom and 7 for lodgers with stabling for 6 horses and 6 vehicles.

In 1932 Lindsells became part of Huntingdon Breweries Ltd, which in turn became part of East Anglian Breweries in 1950. The license was surrendered on 4th March 1954 and the Railway Tavern closed. The property was demolished and the site is now part of an agricultural engineering firm.

1850 - 1851 Levi Hardiment	1926 - 1930 John Bernard Scarfe
1851 - 1872 Walter Womack	1931 - 1934 James Bartell
1873 - 1875 Henry Womack	1935 - 1935 Joseph Benjamin Whillock
1876 No return	1936 - 1939 William Hewitt
1877 - 1882 Mrs Mary Ann Womack	1940 - 1946 John William Lockwood
1883 - 1906 Wortham Hitch	1947 - 1954 Nellie Rose Lockwood
1907 - 1925 Jim Chapman	

RED LION

The former Red Lion Inn as it is in 2007.

The Red Lion Inn stood mid way on the north side of High Street. The building is still in existence, though much altered and is today a travel Agent and a key cutting shop.

It is obviously of the 17th century or earlier, for it was already established as an inn in 1636, when Mary Smythe, a widow of Ely, and her daughter laid information before John Goodericke, Justice of the Peace, against two Ely labourers for burglary. William Papworth, junior, and Thomas Burton were charged that on "*Sunday being Christmas daye the xxvth daye of December 1636, betwixt the hours of two or three of the clock in the afternoon*" Mary and all the rest of the household were at "*devyne service*". William Papworth, together with Thomas Burton, it was alleged "*did beate downe a Baye which he did cutt with a morespade, a hammer and a paire of pynsers; dyd breake open two lockes, the one of a trunke and the other of a chest wherein her money did lye. And took out x pounds in gould , twenty in silver and xxxtie single pence, all which money was taken in the pocket of the said William Papworth att house of Mrs Key, hostys at the Redd Lyon in Ely*".

It was in 1728 that Elizabeth Stoughton, of Bottisham, came to Ely and "*lay at the Red Lyon inn....; that some time after she had gone to bed and fallen asleep she was suddenly awakened by one John Green of Downham in Norfolk, Sider merchant. That the said John Green came into her bedroom whilst she was asleep; that when awake she perceived his arms about her neck; that he attempted to pull off the Bedcloaths from her and ly with here; that crying out he left her and went out of the room and made no further attempt upon her. And this Deponent further saith that some time after the same night or towards Morning* she meet with the like attempt upon her chastity from James Shades of Newmarket, Innkeeper, and rescued herself from him by the like crying out".

In May 1763 the Trustees of the Turnpike Road met at the house of Elizabeth Jeffery known "*by the sign of the Red Lyon in Ely*". Later in the year, on 5th October, they met at "*the house of Mr. Worth Marshall, known by the sign of the Red Lyon in Ely*". Worth Marshall continued at the inn until at least 1780. During the next 30 years the Turnpike Trustees held their meeting here.

It is interesting to note the Red Lion's literary associations. In his account of the Ely Pamphlet Club, John Feather writes, " *On 9 January 1766 a group of twelve men met at the Red Lion in Ely to establish their club, and to draw up rules for its conduct. The rules regulated the purchase, loan and sale of the books. There were to be no more than twelve members, each of whom was to pay 2s. 6d. a quarter to the steward, whom they elected from among themselves. The club was to meet at the Red Lion, On alternate Thursday evenings between 6 and 8, and books were to be purchased after a majority vote at a meeting ... Although books could be borrowed only on club nights, a key to the room in which they were kept was deposited with the landlord of the Red Lion, and members had the right of access at any time for the Liberty of perusing*". While the club was flourishing the steward was the landlord, Worth Marshall. He was also a "*Singing Man*" of the Cathedral, as the Lay Clerks were then known.

The inn must have had a reputation for its food since on the occasion when the United Volunteers of Ely, Stretham and Haddenham, under Lieutenant Colonel Brackenbury, were reviewed and inspected at Ely in 1804, Brigadier General Stewart and Sir Edward Baines dined with the officers at the Red Lion Inn.

The Red Lion was auctioned on 2nd October 1815 when Mrs Ann Reynolds retired. An advert for another auction of the Red Lion on 30 November 1837 described the property as "*situated in the centre of the High St of Ely, including a confectioner's shop, they occupy a frontage of 55ft next the High St, are 134ft in depth, and 38 feet in width at the back entrance, and consist of a Market Room next the street, of 17ft by 15ft, a large dining room 37 ft in length, and nearly 16ft in width, a small dining room adjoining, a good Bar, a Shop and Premises, two Parlours, seven Bedrooms, two Kitchens, a Spacious Brewing Office, good Cellerage, Coal House, large Yard, Stabling for 20 Horses, excellent Granaries, Hay and Straw Lofts and there is a Pump of excellent spring water in the Yard. The above premises are well adapted for a spirited person who would brew superior Beer, and conduct the business of the House respectfully. They have been well known as a good accustomed Inn and Market House for upward of two Centuries*".

In 1823, Pigot & Co's directory was advertising the "Royal Mail" coach departing from the Red Lion for Cambridge every evening at six o'clock.

By 1858 the Inn became the property of Hugh Robert Evans, a solicitor, who came to Ely from Wales. By 1872 James Home had taken over as landlord, but by this time Charles Mainprice owned the inn and it was described by then as "*wine & spirit merchants*".

HOME & Co.,
Wine Merchants, &c.,
HIGH STREET, ELY.

BASS & Co.'s ALES are sent out in sound and brilliant condition in bottles (qts. and pts.) and in casks (18 and 9 galls.) Brewed from PURE MALT and HOPS only.

IN BOTTLES.

	per doz. pts.	per doz. qts.
BASS & CO.'S INDIAN PALE ALE	3/6	7/-
GUINNESS' STOUT	3/6	6/6
BASS' STOUT	2/6	5/-
BASS' & CO.'S LIGHT ALE	2/-	4/-
CHAMPAGNE CIDER	4/-	8/-

Trueman & Co.'s INVALID STOUT, in 9 gall. casks, at 1/8 per gall.

Sherries, Ports, Australian Wines, Clarets, Champagne, and all Light Wines.

St. JULIEN CLARET, at 18/- and 24/- per doz.

Brandy (pale & brown), Gin, Whiskey, Rum, & Liqueurs. All of the best quality.

CIGARS OF THE BEST BRAND.

Home & Co.'s Scotch Whiskey, "GLENLIVET," carefully blended is a great success, because the Public find it a genuine wholesome and palatable beverage, thoroughly matured.

John Jameson & Son's well-known Irish Whiskey is also a great success, because the Public find it a well matured and pure Spirit.

A LIST OF PRICES ON APPLICATION.

An advert from the Ely Red Book of 1902.

During the renovation of the Green Dragon in Chesterton in May 1962 a printed card was found, which read " *ELY MAIL CART, The public are respectfully informed that the ELY MAIL, for Conveyance of Goods and Parcels, starts from Witt's House, St. Andrew's Street, every Morning at Half-past Six, and arrives at the Red Lion, Ely, at Nine, returns at Five, and arrives at Cambridge at Half-past Seven in the Evening. Goods conveyed as cheap as by Carrier or Coach*". William Witt.

During the turn of the 20th century Mr Home was an agent for the Bass Brewing Company. The Red Lion held a full alehouse license until it was dropped in 1911 upon the closure of the Inn.

1636 - Mrs Key	1815 - 1837 Thomas Johnson
- 1763 Elizabeth Jeffe	1838 - 1871 Charles Mainprice
1763 - 1780 Worth Marshall	1872 - 1883 James Home
1790 - 1791 William Sholverton	1884 - 1886 James Sedger
1792 - 1802 Abraham Ball	1887 - 1907 James Home
1803 - 1808 Henry Rance	1908 - 1908 William Varrow
1809 - 1814 James Reynolds	1909 - 1909 William Isaac
1815 - 1815 Ann Reynolds	1910 - 1911 Walter S Gibbs

RED, WHITE AND BLUE

These pictures show the earlier building, which was situated on the corner, also the very unusual chimneystack that was at the rear.

The original Red, White and Blue was situated at the corner of Chiefs Street and West Fen Road and during the first half of the 19th century had been known as "*West Fen House*". The original building dated back to 1814 when William Cropley became the owner. After his death the property was sold by auction in July 1852 and described as "*A substantial brick and thatched messauge, being a Beer house called The West Fen House, situate in Chiefs Lane, in Ely Saint Mary's, with yard and outbuildings*", and purchased by John Muriel, Surgeon who was admitted in 1853. In 1857 he entered into an agreement to sell to William Harlock, gentleman, for £450. By this time the property was described as "*All that customary or copy-hold Messuage or Tenement situate at the corner of Chiefs Lane and Cow Lane in Ely known by the name of the Red White & Blue beer-house*".

During the 1930's in common with many other pubs, it ran a Slate Club for its regular customers.

The Red, White & Blue was licensed as a beer house until February 1950 when that license was transferred to the Coopers' Arms and the ale house license held there was transferred to the Red, White and Blue. The old property was demolished and, in 1965, a new one built, set back several yards from the site of the original, which stood on the corner. On 21st October 1965 an application for off sales was added to the license.

The Red, White and Blue was closed in 1998 and demolished by mid 2000 to make way for a new housing development now called Bakers Court.

The site of the former Red, White and Blue in 2007.

1864 - 1867 Charles Hitch
1869 - 1887 William Neal
1888 - 1899 William Neal Jnr.
1900 - 1908 William Green
1908 - 1911 James Fitch
1912 - 1914 Mrs Georgina Fitch
1915 - 1942 Ebenezer Harold Fitch
1942 - 1957 Mrs.Laura Fitch

1957 - 1971 Leonard Arthur Pettitt
1971 - 1979 Dudley Nathan Lovett
1979 - 1986 Percy Scott
1987 - 1990 John Anthony David Perry
1991 - 1991 Geoffrey Pridmore
1992 - 1992 Brian Raymond Audus
1992 - 1993 Maria Patricia Burgess
1993 - 1998 Ann Morriss.

RIFLEMAN (Volunteer)

The former Rifleman during the mid 1900's and the site in 2007.

On the corner of Back Hill and Broad Street once stood the Rifleman, or Volunteer as it was often known. It was likely to have taken its name from the Ely Rifle Volunteer Corps, which was formed in 1860.

It is known that beer was being sold from the premises as early as 1853 as in the 26th February edition of the Cambridge Chronicle, it was reported "*On Monday last, person or persons broke into the dwelling house of Mrs Ellis Hills, general shop keeper and retailer of beer, corner of Broad St in the City*", whether it was called the Rifleman then is unclear. However it was known as the Rifleman by 1867 and it held a beer house license. The landlords had other trades to supplement their income, which was common at this time, as the sale of beer alone would not provide sufficient revenue. Ellis Hills was listed as baker & grocer, Robert Annison was also shown as a baker and William Buckle as a shopkeeper.

On 6th April 1880 a new licence was applied for when the previous one had lapsed due to the vacation of Robert Annison.

In 1906 the premises were shown to have 3 bedrooms for the licensee's use and 2 for lodgers but no stabling was provided.

The Rifleman was owned by the Hill's family of Cambridge and leased to Thomas Legge, brewer of Ely, until 1912, when it was taken over by Cutlack & Harlock. It closed in 1916 under the 1904 compensation scheme.

1853 - Ellis Hills	1883 - 1899 William Buckle
1866 - 1879 Robert Annison	1900 - 1902 William Hoxley
1880 - 1880 John Ellis	1903 - 1905 John Dunham
1880 - 1882 Alfred Raby	1906 - 1916 William Buckle
1882 - 1883 Sarah Ann Raby	

RISING SUN

The former Rising Sun in the 1960's and the site as it is in 2007.

Built by local builder Obediah Cross in 1847, the Rising Sun once stood at number 47, Prickwillow Road, formerly Common Lane.

The first record of it becoming a public house was in 1850 when it was licensed as a beer house and as such could not sell wines or spirits, until 7th February 1952, when the alehouse license was transferred from the now closed Wheatsheaf.

The Rising Sun was owned and supplied by Henry Hall's brewery and remained in the Hall's family until merger with Cutlack & Harlock in 1930.

In 1906 it was listed as having 1 bedroom for the licensee's family and 3 for Lodgers, with stabling for 1 horse. During the 1930's, in common with many of the City's pubs, the Rising Sun ran a Slate Club for its regulars.

Closure of the Rising Sun came on the 4th February 1969 by the then owner Steward & Patteson, although the license was still held and not surrendered until 4th March 1971. The property was demolished and new housing now occupies the site.

1850 - 1876 Robert Poole	1909 - 1909 A C Westley
1877 - 1879 John Henry Onion	1910 - 1912 George Norman
1880 - 1888 James Daisley	1913 - 1923 William Cross
1888 - 1891 Richard Atkin Jnr	1923 - 1931 Walter Beamiss
1891 - 1902 Daniel Clerk	1932 - 1941 Frank William Plumb
1903 - 1905 Alfred Barton	1941 - 1946 Mrs Plumb
1906 - 1908 Thomas Maynard Barley	1946 - 1971 Frank William Plumb

ROSE AND CROWN

The Rose and Crown during the 1960's and the property as it is in 2007.

Situated on the South side of Fore Hill was the Rose and Crown. On 23rd August 1848 at the annual licensing meeting, James Cuttriss had his license suspended for a week, along with his other brothers, to "*allow the magistrates time to consider the most desirable steps to be taken to stop the torrent of vice and infamy consequent upon the irregular and improper manner in which he conducted his house*". The landlord in 1865 was R J Sydal, who was charged on 16th March for "*permitting disorderly conduct in his house*", the following year he didn't have his license renewed. Mary Negus must also have run a house of some ill repute, as on 19th November 1876 she was fined £2 with £1 costs for permitting drunkenness and on 16th April 1878 she was charged for "*allowing prostitutes to remain in premises longer than was necessary for reasonable refreshment*", no doubt this would have contributed to her annual license not being renewed.

In 1906 the Rose & Crown was listed as providing its landlord with 2 bedrooms and 3 for lodgers though no stabling was provided. It held a full alehouse license until its closure in February 1969, by Steward & Patteson. The property is now an Indian Restaurant.

1790 - 1799 John Rowlett	1876 - 1878 Mary Negus
1800 - 1828 John Jarman	1879 - 1879 George Wham
1829 - 1835 Mary Jarman	1880 - 1880 Thomas Few
1836 - 1850 James Cuttriss	1881 - 1881 E W Harlock
1851 - 1854 William Ringer	1882 - 1929 William Bailey
1855 - 1855 Thomas Sindell	1929 - 1929 Herbert Charles Bailey
1856 - 1856 Thomas Stones	1929 - 1931 Edward Henry Buige
1857 - 1857 Fredrick Lyon	1932 - 1932 Bartholemew Kiley
1858 - 1861 Henry Willson	1932 - 1934 Albert William Long
1862 - 1862 Raymond Thos Forestall	1934 - 1936 Leonard Frank Folland
1863 - 1865 Richard Jenkyns Sydal	1936 - 1948 George Leonard Bobbett
1866 - 1875 John Hobbs	1949 - 1957 Fredrick James Parr
1876 - 1876 Stephen Hay	1957 - 1970 Thomas William Balmer

ROUND OF BEEF

The Round of Beef in the 1930's shortly before closure and the site in 2007.

The Round of Beef stood at the junction of Fore Hill and Broad Street, next to the main entrance of Hall's new Brewery.

In October 1856 Ann Dooler was charged with "*having her house open for the sale of beer before half past twelve on Sunday 19th for which she was fined 20s and 10s costs*". Ann later married Edward Moll and they ran the pub together until Edward died, when she became landlady once more.

Licensed as a beer house, the Baron was supplied and owned by Thomas Legge's brewery until 1910, when it was taken over by Cutlack & Harlock.

In 1906 it was listed as providing its landlord with 6 bedrooms, 3 of which were for lodgers and stabling for one horse.

The Round of Beef was closed by 1937 and later demolished to make way for a new, grand entrance to Hall, Cutlack & Harlock's brewery. The site is now a private residence, numbers 43 & 45 Fore Hill.

1850 - 1851 Robert Osbourne
1856 - 1858 Ann Dooler
1859 - 1867 Edward Moll
1869 - 1883 Ann Moll

1883 - 1887 George Dobson
1888 - 1919 William Newby
1919 - 1935 Mrs Ruth Newby

ROYAL OAK

The Royal Oak in the 1920's and the property as it is in 2007.

One of three pubs on the junction of Back Hill and Broad Street, the Royal Oak was number 78, Back Hill, on the corner with Potters Lane.

The property must have had a substantial amount of land attached to it, as William Cave Cranwell was listed in directories of the time, as being landlord of the Royal Oak also farmer, market gardener & seedsman.

Landlord William Buckle was well known to the authorities as he was twice before the magistrates, firstly on 1st August 1875 when *"Wm Buckle of the Royal Oak, keeping house open for the sale of beer at 8.30'* for which he was fined £5 with costs and his license endorsed, then again on 17th April 1880 when *"Wm Buckle of the Royal Oak, opening his house for sale of beer after 11pm"* this time he was fined £1 with 14/6 costs.

In 1875 the Royal Oak was owned and supplied by E W Harlock's brewery and remained a Harlock's house until the merger with Cutlack's brewery in 1907. In 1906 it was shown to provide the landlord with 3 bedrooms and 2 for lodgers with stabling for 2 horses and 2 vehicles. During the 1930's the Royal Oak ran a Thrift Club for its regular customers.

The Royal Oak held a full alehouse license up to its closure by East Anglian Breweries on 15th December 1958. Today it is a private residence called Royal Oak House.

1786 - 1790 Edward Bromfield
1791 - 1795 Thomas Bartle
1796 - 1798 John Bartle
1799 - 1812 Thomas Munson
1813 - 1814 William Munson
1815 - 1815 Robert Davey
1816 - 1817 Elizabeth Spakeman

1861 - 1862 William James Haylock
1863 - 1870 William Fenn
1871 - 1871 Henry Willson
1872 - 1884 William Buckle
1885 - 1885 Robert Whitehead
1886 - 1886 James Adkins
1887 - 1899 William Drage

1818 - 1831 Thomas Bartingale	1900 - 1916 King Spinks
1832 - 1843 William Rust	1916 - 1917 William Buckle
1844 - 1850 Martha Rust	1918 - 1935 Elizabeth Vincent Buckle
1851 - 1852 Cophas Cotterell	1936 - 1937 Walter Beamiss
1853 - 1858 William. Cave Cranwell	1938 - 1938 Edward Henry Buige
1859 - 1859 Joseph Chapman	1939 - Rhoda Gray
1860 - 1860 Joseph South	1947 - 1958 Mrs Rhoda Harris

ROYAL STANDARD

FT Cross's "Ye olde Tea Rooms", later to become part of the current Royal Standard, with the original Standard beyond, displaying a sign advertising Morgans of Norwich, Ales and Stouts.

The Royal Standard is situated mid-way up Fore Hill and is today a larger premises than when it first opened. Probably called the Baron of Beef, (the same as the establishment across the road, run by Joseph Nightingale) as the license returns show William Toombs at the Baron of Beef in 1876 then in 1877 Michael Howe was licensed, both having the owner as Ekins Augustine. The Standard opened as a beer house occupying the part toward the bottom of the hill, of the building that we see today. William Toombs had a brush with the local constabulary when he was charged with "*Opening house during prohibited hours* " on Sunday 21st May 1878, though the charge was dismissed at court but he had to pay costs. In 1887 Joseph Laurence was charged with "*unlawfully allowing drunkenness in his house on 10th September*".

The 1906 Returns of Licensed Houses showed that the "Standard" had 3 bedrooms for the licensee's use and 3 for lodgers but no stabling also that the landlord, Mr Emery had been charged with "*Permitting Drunkenness on 18th June 1903*" for which he was fined £3 and £2/12/6 costs.

By 1914 a change in ownership had taken place from William Samuel Giscard to Morgan, the Norwich brewers, who in turn had sold it by 1929 to Greene King. Along with many other pubs in Ely during the 1930's the "Standard" ran a Slate Club for its regulars.

As recently as 1965, during Mr Ratcliffe's tenure as landlord, a license for the sale of wines and spirits was applied for and granted by the court.

In 1969 the Standard was extended to include the next building up the hill which was formerly the noted tearoom run by the Cross family for many years. As well as being a tearoom, it housed a unique collection of local and natural history exhibits, which eventually became the nucleus of the Ely Museum. The Standard is still open today and continues as a Green King house.

1871 - 1871 Charles Cole	1903 - 1910 George Arthur Emery
1872 - 1877 William Toombs	1911 - 1911 Charles George Griffin
1878 - 1880 Michael Howe	1912 - 1913 Berkeley Smith
1880 - 1880 Michael Norton	1914 - 1914 Walter Parker Jnr
1880 - 1881 George Symonds	1915 - 1916 Hugh Butty
1881 - 1881 John Dodds	1917 - 1923 Edgar Burrows
1882 - 1882 William Bone	1923 - 1923 William John Glass
1883 - 1884 Walter Newton	1924 - 1929 Edward Henry Buige
1884 - 1886 William Herbert Garner	1929 - 1965 Herbert Richard Harrison
1886 - 1888 Joseph Lawrence	1965 - 1973 Tom Ratcliffe
1888 - 1889 William Henry Webb	1973 - 1978 Kevin Roy Francis
1889 - 1891 William Wilson	1979 - 1980 Micheal Frank Grove
1891 - 1892 Thomas Pate	1980 - 1994 Francis Alwyn King
1893 - 1899 John Butcher	1994 - 2007 Brian Patrick McDermott
1900 - 1902 Isaac Redhead	2007 - Curr. Richard Whitmore

SHIP

The Ship Inn during the early 1900's.

The Ship Inn was situated on the corner of Ship Lane and the Quayside. In 1661 a license was granted to John Knowles who, in 1667 issued tokens with a ship depicted on one side. During 1666 the wife of John Knowles, Ann, was accused of " *Abusing of constables in the executing of their office*". Later, in 1786, it is recorded that Robert Fox who was tenant, was paying an annual rent of £11 and a rate of 16s.6d.

In 1775 one Tinkler, Currier of Norwich, announced in the Cambridgeshire Chronicle that he had opened a "*house for all sorts of curried leather*" at the Ship. During the early1800s the Ship was frequently used for holding inquests and public auctions where river tradesmen would sell their wares.

In December 1811 it was the inn itself that was under the auctioneer's hammer. Lot1 consisted of "*All those, truly valuable old-established extensive PREMISES, comprising the SHIP INN, with a complete brewing-office, inn room, and other requisite buildings for that purpose; very good granary, 4 stables capable of containing 90 horses, three warehouses contiguous to the River Ouse, with an excellent quay for the delivery of merchandize, large roomy yard and stack ditto, with lodges etc, a garden well planted with choice fruit trees, also a respectable Tenement*".

In April 1854 a " *Fire at the Ship Inn, Quay Side, On Saturday night-last, between 10 and 11 o'clock, a fire broke out, and consumed a very valuable hay stack and a lodge adjoining. An alarm was given and plenty of help was readily afforded*". "*Thomas Ward, a tramp, from Buntingford, was apprehended by Sergeant Heard, on suspicion of setting fire to the stack. He had been seen at the Ship, under not very satisfactory circumstances*".

The Returns of Licensed Houses described the Ship as having 3 bedrooms for the landlord's use and one for lodgers with stabling for 8 horses.

In 1858 it was owned by Ebenezer Harlock, as it was advertised in the Cambridge Chronicle of 20th February that year as being "*TO LET, THE SHIP, Old Licensed Public House, situate on the Quay-side Ely, Immediate Possession maybe had. Apply to Harlock and Sons, Brewery Ely*". It remained a Harlock's house until mergers of the early 1900's. East Anglian Breweries Ltd closed it in 1955. By 1961 the Ship had been demolished, the site is now part of the riverside walk and a green. The crane that once stood outside the Ship was moved and now stands on the opposite side of the river at the entrance to the marina.

1661 - 1667 John Knowles	1881 - 1885 Caroline Brown
1786 - 1797 Robert Fox	1886 - 1897 Edward Cooper
1798 - 1802 Ann Fox	1898 - 1900 Thomas Chevell
1803 - 1811 Charles Boyce	1901 - 1902 George Ellis
1812 - 1816 Robert Griffin	1903 - 1907 Richard Ready Smith
1817 - 1824 Mary Griffin	1908 - 1920 Jacob Venney
1825 - 1857 James Griffin	1921 - 1921 Sophia Venney
1858 - 1858 Elijah Attlesey	1921 - 1929 Herbert Cuthbert Childs
1859 - 1877 Robert Black	1930 - 1955 Alfred Viney
1878 - 1880 James Brown	

STAR

The site of the former Star public house in 2007.

The Star was located on the junction of Newnham Street and Nutholt Lane at number 26, and was only licensed for the sale of beer.

An advertisement in the Cambridge Chronicle announced "*To Brewer's, Publicans and Others. Desirable situation for a Public-House In Newnham, Ely. To Be Sold By Auction by Geo.Legge. At the King's Arms, in-Ely on Thursday 5th October 1848 at seven o'clock in the evening. All that desirable and substantially built Brick and Tiled messuage, with a Cottage adjoining and a Piece of Land behind, situate in Newnham, Ely, being the corner house with Two Frontages, 49ft on the West, 49ft on the North, lately occupied by Mr Edward Luddington. The above Premises are eligibly situated for a Public House being next to the Cattle Market and adjoining the Principle entrance to Ely from the fen*" It is understood this was to become the Star beer house. Thomas Legge, Brewer of Ely, purchased the property and supplied beer to the pub. The 1906 Returns of Licensed Houses credited the Star with 3 bedrooms for the licensee and unusually none for lodgers and no stabling. In 1910 the then owners, Hall, Cutlack & Harlock leased this property, and in 1922 purchased it from the owner Rev Alfred Legge.

The Star ran a Slate Club for its customers in the last couple of years before its closure in 1932, when the then Isle of Ely County Council bought a parcel of land from Hall, Cutlack & Harlock comprising of the "*former beer house known as The Star and two adjacent cottages Numbers 28 & 30 Newnham Street*" for the purpose of highway improvement. These properties were subsequently demolished and the corner re-aligned; a carpet shop now stands approximately on the site.

1850 - 1851 William Partridge
1864 - 1869 William Smith
1869 - 1880 William Clark
1880 - 1906 Benjamin Curtis
1907 - 1915 Mrs Sarah Ann Curtis
1916 - 1932 John Potts Butler

SUN

The former Sun public house in 2007.

Originally the Sun was situated on the north side of Market Street between Newnham Street and the White Hart Hotel, next to Legge's Brewery, as shown in a trade directory of 1867. Between 1794 and 1847 it is likely the license was changed from an alehouse to beer house license, for which records then were not kept or the pub had closed for that period. In 1887 the Sun moved premises after *"An application by Elizabeth Buttress of the Sun Beer House Ely Trinity for the removal of the license from her present house to the premises lately occupied by Wm Allison in Market Street Ely"*, was made on the 24th August, this was duly granted. The "new" Sun was listed as being at 19, Market Street which is on the south side, however Market Street has been renumbered since then and it is now number 31. Two years later she was in court on 1st August 1889, when she was charged with *"knowingly permitting drunkenness in her house on 25th July 1889"* for which she was fined.

In 1906 the Sun was listed as having 2 bedrooms for the landlords use and 1 for lodgers with no stabling.

Licensed as a beer house, the Sun was supplied by Legge's brewery, until 1910 when Legge's merged with Cutlack & Harlock. The license was dropped in 1927 and the property today is a shoe shop.

1790 - 1794 Daniel Clark	1894 - 1900 Joseph Lawrence
1847 - 1851 Francis Woods	1900 - 1906 Joseph Bruce
1851 - 1858 Thomas Legge	1907 - 1909 Joseph Lawrence
1864 - 1875 Christopher Buttress	1910 - 1925 Alfred Harnwell
1876 - 1893 Elizabeth Buttress	

THREE BLACKBIRDS

The former Three Blackbirds in 2007.

Number 41, Broad Street was once the Three Blackbirds Inn, which held an "old" alehouse license. Whenever the premises became known as the Three Blackbirds is not recorded, but its life as a public house was obviously but a small part of its history.

In 1796 Mrs Howe, keeper of the inn, was returning, "*sincere thanks to her friends and the public in general for the past favours conferred upon her late husband Mr Richard Howe*" and was begging to inform them that she intended carrying on the "*business of the Inn, and of the Lime-Kilns belonging to the premises*" and soliciting "*their future commands & favours; assuring them that nothing shall be wanting on her part to accommodate them in either of the above branches*". Six months later the widow "*declined the business*" and was advertising the auction in the Cambridge Chronicle of December 31st, "*To be sold by Auction - 3 Jan 1797 by T.Wetenhall. The Neat and Genuine HOUSEHOLD FURNITURE, Plate, Linen, Glass, China and other effects of Mrs ANN HOWE, at the Three Black Birds, Ely (who has declined business).....*".

During the Littleport and Ely riots of 1816, the rioters attacked the baker's shop opposite, when the son of the baker, William Rickwood, offered the mob "*beer at the Blackbirds*".

The Three Blackbirds was again up for auction on 8th August 1839 and described as "*consisting of all that old-fashioned and well accustomed Free Public House, with extensive yard, in which are stables for 10 Horses, Brewhouse, Large Barn used as a Boatwrights shop, Granary, Limekiln in full trade, a thriving Orchard well planted with young Trees, and a Garden the whole containing One Acre and a half*".

On 23rd August 1848 at the annual licensing meeting, William Cuttriss had his license suspended for a week, along with his other brothers, to "*allow the magistrates time to consider the most desirable steps to be taken to stop the torrent of vice and infamy consequent upon the irregular and improper manner in which he conducted his house*".

William was again before the magistrates on 23rd October 1859 when he was charged with 2 counts of having "*deficient measures*" for which he was fined 5s and 12.6d costs.

By 1875 the "Blackbirds" was in the hands of Henry Hall, and remained with the family until 1930 when they merged with Cutlack & Harlock. In 1906 the inn provided its landlord with 3 bedrooms and 4 for lodgers with stabling for 2 horses. The license was dropped by 1933 and the inn became a private residence. In 1981 the Ely Preservation Trust took over the ownership and after a restoration and conversion programme the Blackbirds was put on the market in 1984.

1790 - 1792 Mary Foulgham	1871 - 1892 John Brown
1793 - 1795 Richard Howe	1892 - 1894 Mrs Martha Brown
1796 - 1796 Ann Howe	1895 - 1896 Henry Oakman
1797 - 1806 Thomas Andrews	1897 - 1898 Robert Oakes
1807 - 1807 Elizabeth Andrews	1899 - 1901 George Bruce
1808 - 1815 James Bal	1902 - 1905 John Bates
1816 - 1824 Edward Ingram	1906 - 1907 Benjamin Oakman
1825 - 1825 Ann Spenceley	1908 - 1908 William Leonard Horton
1826 - 1826 Robert Cuttriss	1909 - 1912 Arthur A Peachey
1827 - 1845 Thomas Wilkin	1913 - 1925 John William Smith
1846 - 1847 Elizabeth Wilkin	1925 - 1925 John Layton
1848 - 1860 William Cuttriss	1926 - 1931 Fredrick Brown
1861 - 1870 Thomas Appleyard	1931 - 1932 J Burton

THREE CROWNS

One of the largest buildings in the Waterside area stands at Crown Point and was, until 1912, the Three Crowns public house. The present building, number 31, is mainly 18th century and faces onto Waterside. The adjoining building was a Smithy, which was a source of additional income for many of the landlords of the Three Crowns.

It was in a building on this site that "*Oliver Cromwell Esq*" was elected a governor of Parsons' Charity in 1636. After the death of his maternal uncle, Sir Thomas Steward of Stuntney Old Hall, Cromwell came to live in Ely at the present Oliver Cromwell's House for ten or eleven years.

In the next century the premises were described in the will of Susannah Robinson, dated 1771, as having "*Brewhouse, Storehouse, Yards Gardens & Appurts.*" It was at this time in "*the Tenure or Occupation of John Harlock of Ely aforesaid, Yeoman, his undertenants or Assigns.*" Soon after this John Harlock bought the property for the sum of £422 and he and his heirs appear to have owned it into the 1900's. Its history is confused by the fact that by 1825 it was divided and part of it described as "*All that Messauge now converted into two cottages*". This was when Benjamin Feast, blacksmith, was landlord. Further structural alterations appear to have been made as it was later referred to as being "*lately converted into 3 tenements in the occupation of William Fuller, Thomas Clay & William Theobald*".

The former Three Crowns during the 1950's.

Thomas Willson was charged on 12th November 1842 with "*Breach of Alehouse license, Victualler licensed to Three Crowns in Ely, keeping the same in a disorderly manner*" the charge was withdrawn on payment of £1/3/6.

An article in the Ely gazette on 3rd October 1890 reported that "*An application by Ellis King of the Three Crowns public house, Waterside, for that establishment to be registered as a common lodging house, and was agreed to*". In 1906 it provided 2 bedrooms for the landlord and 3 for lodgers but no stabling. Ellis King and members of his family continued to live at the Three Crowns long after it closed in 1912 under the 1904 compensation scheme.

1790 - 1800 John Smith	1815 - 1825 Benjamin Feast
1801 - 1806 Edward Smith	1826 - 1860 Thomas Willson
1807 - 1813 James Dawson	1861 - 1875 William Benton
1814 - 1814 William Harlock	1876 - 1912 Ellis King

THREE CUPS

The former Three Cups Inn as it is in 2007.

Situated at the top of Fore Hill, the Three Cups was one of a number of inns that surrounded the Market Place. The Georgian building hides a structure within its fabric, which dates back to the 17th Century. There is reference to the Three Cups in an entry in the Parsons' Charity Accounts book of 1688.
1st February "*Expended at a meeting at the 3 Cups 5s 10d*".
2nd April "*Expended at a meeting at the 3 Cups 5s 2d*".
The passageway next to the premises was named Three Cups Walk as a reminder of this ancient inn.

TINKER OF ELY

Along Lynn Road on the old Turnpike Road from Ely to Kings Lynn is an area, which used to be known as Little London and where once stood the Tinker of Ely public house. A sketch plan drawn up shortly after 1752, when the Turnpike Road had been established, shows the Tinker with its projecting signboard, also that the original frontage of the cottages in Little London stood back some distance from the existing Lynn Road. Some of the cottages remain showing a long garden in front of them.

In 1840 Christopher Thurston had obtained possession, and he sold part of the property to Phoebe Rayner, widow, for £200, but the rest of the property was sold in 1842 to William Harlock, the elder, Common Brewer and it is described as "*all that messuage or dwelling house called the Tinker of Ely*". In 1850 Christopher Thurston, described as a brickmaker, mortgaged the pub to Mary and Charlotte King of Tadlow, Cambs. It was described as "*a dwelling house used as a public house, sign of the Tinker of Ely, in tenure of Christopher Thurston. A brew-house adjoining, but not connecting*".

In 1859, John Darling, beer house keeper was charged *"with having his house open for sale of beer before half past twelve o'clock"* on Sunday 10th July*.

The Tinker changed its name in 1860 to the Rifleman's Arms, in recognition of the newly mustered Ely Rifle Volunteers who, in 1861, had a shooting range nearly opposite the Inn. The range was 600 yards long and an old railway carriage served as storage for the targets and butt registers. The range ceased to be used after the First World War, but has left its mark in the name "Butts Drove".

An article in the Ely Weekly Gazette reported that William S Darling was summoned for *"knowingly allowing drunkenness in his house"* on 31st August 1890. *"William Reeves said that on the day named he saw a man named Hobbs the worse for beer, but not drunk, in the defendants house. P.C. Vails stated that he lived near the Riflemans Arms and about 1.45 on the 30th of August he saw the man Hobbs coming from the defendant's premises, whilst in charge of a horse and cart, in such a condition that he thought it advisable to take him into custody. Defendant admitted that he and his wife drew a pint of beer each for the man Hobbs, Mr Allen representing Messrs Hall, brewers, explained that arrangements had been made for another tenant to take the house.- Defendant was ordered to pay the expenses, £1.3s. A temporary transfer of the license was afterwards made to Mr Ralph Boness, formally of the Bell Tap"*.

Another landlord in trouble with the law was Harry Carpenter, who was fined 5/- with 11/- costs *"for opening his house for the sale of beer to pretended travellers"* on Sunday 3rd November 1895.

In 1906 the Inn provided its landlord with 3 bedrooms and 3 for lodgers with stabling for 3 horses and during the 1930's a Slate Club was run for its regulars.

Landlord Albert Reginald Seekings was a true hero, born in Stuntney 1920, nobody back home knew of the top-secret work he did during the Second World War. He joined the Cambridgeshire Regiment (Volunteers) at 18 years of age, later he was one of the first to volunteer for Lt Col Stirling's new Special Air Service. As a founder member of the S.A.S he saw action in North Africa, Italy and the D-Day landings in Normandy. He was also the first allied soldier to cross the threshold of the Belsen concentration camp. During his service he earned a raft of 11 Second World War medals. He achieved the rank of Squadron Sergeant-Major before returning to Cambridgeshire where he became landlord of the Rifleman's Arms.

In 1972 considerable improvements were made to the inn and a new bar was installed. At the official opening the first pint was drawn by Warrant Officer Bates of the Royal Anglian Regiment.

1990 saw the Rifleman's Arms change its name back to the Tinker of Ely.

Along with many other pubs the original Tinker brewed its own beer on the premises but by 1874 it was supplied by Henry Hall's brewery and up to the mergers of the mid 1900's, eventually becoming a Watney pub and finally passing to Swann Inns. It was originally licensed as a beer house until 3rd February 1937, when the Spirit license was transferred from the Maid's Head, allowing the Tinker to sell beers, ales, wines and spirits for the first time. The property was demolished in 1999 and new houses were built on the site, numbers 142 and 144 Lynn Road.

1840 - 1851 Charles Thurston
1858 - 1883 John Darling
1883 - 1889 Mrs Ann Darling
1890 - 1890 William Samuel Darling
1890 - 1894 Ralph Boness
1895 - 1896 Henry Carpenter
1897 - 1902 Richard Atkin
1903 - 1912 Mrs Ann Ellingham
1913 - 1924 Harry King
1925 - 1938 Harry Ashmore
1939 - 1940 Bidwell
1941 - 1941 Leonard Lancaster
1942 - 1946 Mrs Alice Lancaster
1946 - 1954 Albert Reginald Seekings
1955 - 1960 Aubrey Bertram Durrant

1961 - 1965 Fredrick Arthur Bidwell
1966 - 1971 Cyril James Evans
1971 - 1974 John Paul Shepardson
1974 - 1978 Eric John Price
1978 - 1982 R E P Dennis
1983 - 1985 Jim Coulson
1985 - 1988 Denis Frank Colloff
1988 - 1989 Alain Peter Vicerage
1990 - 1990 Anthony Scott Pillow
1991 - 1995 Stephen Eusden
1995 - 1995 Sylvia Jean Taylor
1995 - 1996 Gaynor Long
1996 - 1997 Andrew David Handley
1998 - 1998 Ann Hart

TOWN HOUSE

The Town House 2007.

    The Town House is one of Ely's new pubs and situated in Market Street, opened in 1996. The front part of the building was previously used as a Taxi office whilst the main larger back room was a Presbyterian Chapel around the turn of the 20th century. The Town House has enjoyed a flourishing existence as a Free House since opening, in a time when nationally, pubs are closing by the week.

    1996 - Current   Vincent Richard Bartlett

WEST END HOUSE

The West End during the 1960's.

One of Ely's surviving pubs is the West End House, and is situated on the corner of West End and Chief's Street. Originally licensed as a beer house, and as recently as 1954, selling wines and spirits for the first time.

In 1874 Henry Hall was the owner and the pub remained in the Hall family up to the 1930 merger.

Between 1902 and 1903 landlord Henry Morris, whose family were builders and ran the business from the former Eagle Works on Downham Road, was a member of the City Fire Brigade.

In 1906 the West End provided 3 bedrooms for the landlord's use and 1 for lodgers with stabling for 2 horses and 1 vehicle.

As with many other pubs, the West End ran a Slate Club during the 1930's for its regulars. During the Second World War the local Air Raid Wardens met in the Clubroom at the back.

1839 - 1851 Thomas Low	1931 - 1954 Miss Clara Holmes
1853 - 1872 George Morris	1954 - 1965 Harry Brennand
1873 - 1878 Thomas Morley	1965 - 1970 Doris Edith Brennand
1879 - 1885 Thomas William Larkins	1971 - 1975 Winston Fordham
1886 - 1888 Josiah Buckenham	1975 - 1989 Guy Dockerill
1888 - 1891 Joseph Lawrence	1990 - 1995 Geoffrey Pridmore
1892 - 1904 Henry Youngs Morris	1998 - 2002 Vincenzo Teti
1905 - 1931 Edward Albert Holmes	2003 - Curr. Stephen Baxter

WHEATSHEAF

The Wheatsheaf shortly after closure and the property that occupies the site in 2007.

Situated on the junction of West Fen Road (once called Cow Lane) and Downham Road was the Wheatsheaf public house.

Landlady, Elizabeth Hardy, was in breach of her license when she was charged on the 8th November 1851 with "*keeping open Alehouse on a Sunday*".

In Nash & Co's auction of 1852, the Wheatsheaf was listed as Lot 28 and described as "*A Brick and Tile, containing Tap Room, Two Parlours, Cellar, Wash-House, Three Bed Rooms, together with the large YARD and GARDEN, Stables, etc*". A & B Hall purchased the lease for the Wheatsheaf for 343 guineas and it remained a Halls house until the 1930 merger.

In 1864 a Carriers service was advertised from the Wheatsheaf to Cambridge on Wednesdays and Saturdays.

The Pritchard family of Anglesey owned the copyhold for the property. George Pritchard (sheriff of Anglesey) took the additional name of Rayner in 1871 when he married Sarah Mary Brady-Rayner, daughter of John Brady, MP for Ely, Cambridgeshire.

In the 1906 Returns of Licensed houses, the Wheatsheaf is shown to have 2 bedrooms for the licensee's use and 3 for lodgers with stabling for 4 horses and 1 vehicle. Between the war years it ran a Slate Club for its regulars.

The Wheatsheaf closed on 9th February 1952 and the full "old" alehouse license it had held, was transferred to the Rising Sun. The property was demolished and a new residence built, which is known today as Wheatsheaf House.

1790 - 1804 Richard Grantfield	1893 - 1894 Mrs Mary Ann Harle
1805 - 1813 Elizabeth Grantfield	1894 - 1920 James Watson
1814 - 1815 Richard Pikett	1921 - 1935 John Watson
1816 - 1827 Charles Hardy	1936 - 1940 William Collen
1828 - 1852 Mrs Elizabeth Hardy	1940 - 1952 Bertram David Day
1853 - 1892 Edward Harle	

WHEEL

Jessie, Daisy and Ethel Rogers stand in the doorway of their parent's pub and the site of the Wheel in 2007.

The Wheel, also previously known as the Sir Harry Smith, once stood at 13, Broad Street and was licensed as a beer house. Records show that the beer house dated as far back as 1850 when it was called the Sir Harry Smith, named after the distinguished military commander and national hero of the time, having won the battle of Aliwal.

Beer house keeper Fredrick Jacobs, who was also a carrier at the time, was reported in the Cambridge Chronicle of 28th December 1850 as *"appeared for a summons for allowing spirituous liquor to be consumed on his premises. Cautioned and discharged on payment of fines"*.

James Moxon is listed in Kelly's 1858 directory as a *"Wheelwright and beer retailer"* no doubt giving the name to his establishment, whether the pub remained open between 1851 and 1858 is unclear.

On 28th April 1878 landlord George William Owens was fined 10/- and £1 costs for *"permitting drunkenness also 10/- and £1 costs for refusing entry to PC Carter"*. The license was not renewed between 1878 and 1879 as no renewal was applied for at the annual licensing sessions in August 1878, no doubt due to Mr Owens conduct! But a new application was received on 25th September 1879 from a Mr Wilkins for the *"Wheel Beer House"* to Thomas Seaton, which was duly granted.

John Parsons owned the property until 1879 when Mr Ephriam Greaves of Bowes Park, London took ownership. And it remained in the Greaves family until the early 1900s. Cambridge brewer's Bailey & Tebbutt supplied the pub and had a store in the backyard from which they supplied their other houses in the area.

During the early 1900's, the Wheel was one of the pubs in the City to run a fishing club, and between the two world wars it also ran a Slate Club for its regulars.

The 1906 Returns listed the Wheel as having 2 bedrooms for the licensee and 1 for lodgers with stabling for 4 horses and 6 vehicles, no doubt to cater for the brewers business.

The license was dropped in 1942 and the Wheel became an ordinary house. Around 1960 the property was demolished and in 1982 the present house was built.

1850 - 1851 Fredrick Jacobs	1898 - 1900 Walter Martin
1851 - 1855 Philip Rickwood	1901 - 1919 William Rodgers
1858 - 1871 James Moxon	1920 - 1924 Henry John Fordham
1872 - 1878 George William Owens	1925 - 1933 William Joseph Stockbridge
1879 - 1880 Thomas Seaton	
1881 - 1891 Elijah Catchpole	1933 - 1936 George Leonard Bobbit
1891 - 1891 Mary Elizabeth Maltpress (formerly Catchpole)	1936 - 1936 Charles Edwin Perrin
	1937 - 1938 Horace Fredrick Leopold Price
1891 - 1896 James Maltpress	
1896 - 1898 Alfred William Maltpress	1939 - 1942 John Maltman Jackson

WHITE HART

The White Hart Hotel Circa 1870.

Once occupying a prime position on Market Square was the White Hart Inn, it is likely it dates back to the 14th century, it certainly dates back to the following century as it still retains its 15th century timber framing and records of the various undertakings in Ely during the past three hundred years are interspersed with references to the White Hart.

When, in the 17th century, Ely became the centre of the fen drainage operations "*the Conservators of the Bedford Level met at four o'clock in the Whire house on the Market place, but the Jurye being not ready with theyre presentiments the corte adjourned to the White Hart in Ely*".

The Governors of the Land and Possessions of the Poor of Ely (the Feoffees of Parsons' Charity) made frequent use of the accommodation offered by the White Hart both for their annual meeting and for other meetings. When in 1687 the Charity set up a new "*Aspitall in Walpole Lane*" (the establishment was in fact also part school, part workhouse) the landlord of the White Hart made his contribution to the charitable work.

Abraham Byam was evidently a tenant landlord for in her will of 5th May 1730 an Ely widow, Catherine Needham, had bequeathed "*all her lands in Witchford and Wentworth and also her messuage or tenement commonly called the White Hart Inn in Ely with the Cherry Orchard attached, for the establishment of a school and schoolmaster's house*". This was the foundation of the Needham's Charity still in existence today. The will "*appointed eight trustees*" and stipulated that they "*should meet at the White Hart Inn twice in the year and that 20s should be allowed for their dinner*".

By the time John Meadows became landlord in 1813 the White Hart "*lost something of the status it enjoyed for over 150 years*". The Turnpike Trustees, meeting at the nearby Club issued the following statement in 1814, " *The Trustees having reason to be dissatisfied with the Bill delivered in by Mr Meadows, keeper of the White Hart Inn, for the Expense of the meeting held at his house on the 12th of September last. It is hereby Ordered that no more Meetings be holden at the White Hart Inn until further orders*". The Trustees only returned to the inn when William Beecroft took possession '*Mr Meadows having left that house*'. From that time efforts were made to improve the service and reputation of the White Hart.

The depression that settled on agriculture in the years following the Napoleonic Wars resulted in a great deal of unrest in East Anglia and there were disturbances all over the region. The outbreaks of rioting came to a head in the Ely and Littleport riots of 1816. The magistrates were meeting at the White Hart and later a senior magistrate, Revd. Metcalfe, addressed the assembled mob on Market Place from one of the upstairs windows of the Inn, where he issued the statement "*The magistrates agree, and do order, that the over-seers shall pay each family two shillings per head per week, when flour is half a crown a stone; such allowance to be raised in proportion when the price of flour is higher, and that the price of labour shall be two shilling a day, whether married or single and that the labourer shall be paid his full wage by the farmer who hires him*", this met with satisfaction, as after three cheers, many returned to their homes. The magistrates satisfied that trouble was averted foolishly gave out free ale to the remaining crowd, which resulted in the crowd getting drunk and proceeding to commit acts of violence and robbery against many traders in Ely.

In 1838 the owners of the inn, the Needham's Charity Trustees, decided to make considerable improvements, which consisted of an entire new storey comprising five bedrooms. An advert appeared in the Cambridge Chronicle of 6th July 1839 "*Old Established Commercial Inn and Family Hotel, Market Place, Ely,*

Matthew Scott returns thanks to his friends and the public generally for the support he has received nearly eleven years at the above Inn, and respectfully informs them, that during last year (1838) very considerable alterations and improvements were made, by the addition of several airy and comfortable bed and other rooms, now well seasoned (having been occupied some months) and fit for use. The Stable department is greatly enlarged, the buildings and yard on the White Hart premises, formally occupied by the late Mr William Legge, builder, having been fitted up with capital loose and other boxes for the accommodation of 30 horses in addition to the previous extensive stabling, …. The Tea Garden and Bowling-Green , which is respectably attended and conducted, furnishes satisfactory amusement to strangers visiting Ely. The London and Lynn coaches and Mail pass the door daily. A regular supply of genuine Home-brewed Beers and Table Beer, in casks from 36 gallons to 4 ½, Wines and Spirits, selected from the Docks with the greatest care, and no expense spared to secure a good article. Port, 3 years in bottle, fit for table, at £2.2s, Genuine Spirits at reasonable prices". The coming of the Eastern Counties Railway in 1845 no doubt bought Matthew Scott new clients and his horse omnibus attended the arrival and departure of all trains. His advert for the year 1850 shows that the inn was still the posting house for the Mildenhall coach, which left the White Hart every Thursday afternoon at 4 o'clock. Carrier's carts also left his yard for Cambridge, Soham, Southery, Chatteris and Sutton, also, at the White Hart, the Inland Revenue Officer had his office. When Matthew Scott left the White Hart in 1858, George Legge *" was favoured with instructions"* to sell by private contract before 29th Sept. *"An Entire Brewing Plant, containing nearly new Copper, Pumps, Coolers etc. in excellent preservation, about 100 casks, 36 gals each, 4 pockets of Kent hops of first rate quality, 1857 growth. A large wood stable, stalled off, capable of holding 30 horses, with loft above. The gas fittings of the establishment and meter, 20 soldiers Bedsteads and Bedding, a Top boarded floor over an old one, and 2 lights also in soldiers rooms"*.

The new landlord, James Henry Smith, had not been in residence long before he was in trouble with the law, as he was before the magistrates bench on 20th October 1858 *"charged with keeping his house open for the sale of beer at 2am on Sunday"* for which he was fined 10s with 10s costs.

In 1871 the owners sought and obtained authority from the Charity Commision to sell the White Hart. It was advertised as a *"messuage on the Market Place with Court Yard, Private Brewery, Enclosed Garden and Poultry Yard, Bowling Green, Summer House, Stables, Coachhouses and Market Houses; with Tap fronting Newnham"*. It was then in the occupation of William Hodson, a yearly tenant who it seems was brewing his own beer on the premises, however the new owners were themselves brewers, Samuel Gurney Buxton of Catton in Norfolk and John Gurney of Sprowston Hall.

A few years later on the 18th November 1875 William Hudson was fined £2 with £1 costs for *"permitting drunkenness"*. Landlord Walter Moore hadn't held the license long when he too was fined £2 with £1 costs for *"permitting drunkenness"* on 31st January 1878.

In 1891 the White Hart changed owners again, this time the Ely brewers Arthur and Bertram Hall, whose business was rapidly expanding, bought the Inn.

In 1906 the White Hart provided 3 bedrooms for the landlord's use and 8 for lodgers with stabling for 15 horses and 23 vehicles. The inn remained with the Halls until the mid 1900 amalgamations. Under Steward and Patteson the White Hart was completely modernised in 1964.

The White Hart carried an alehouse license throughout its history and finally closed its doors for the last time on the 5th December 1986. The premises were converted for retail use. The former liquor shop and carriage entrance is now a stationers shop whilst the former Commercial room and Coffee room are now a clothing outlet. The words "Hall Cutlack & Harlock Ely" are still discernable on the panel to the right of the upper bay window.

1661 -	Isaac Skinner	1883 - 1883	Joseph Skipper
1722 -	Abraham Byam	1884 - 1894	Ethelbert Bunton Kent
1776 -	Jacob Sallis	1895 - 1895	Richard Jeffrey
1790 - 1812	Thomas Wood	1895 - 1899	Harry Egelton
1813 - 1816	John Meadows	1900 - 1901	Jane Egelton
1817 - 1817	Ann Reynolds	1902 - 1904	Daniel Keeton
1818 - 1827	William Beecroft	1905 - 1905	Walter James Pluck
1828 - 1858	Matthew Scott	1906 - 1914	George Cyris Palmer
1858 - 1864	James Henry Smith	1915 - 1919	Thomas Hood
1865 - 1865	Joseph Pickup	1920 - 1930	John Scarfe
1866 - 1868	James Cheshire	1931 - 1942	James Ernest Cresswell
1869 - 1869	Ann Cheshire	1943 - 1943	Rosetta Martha Burrows
1870 - 1870	Arthur Frank Thomas	1944 - 1953	George William Barwick
1871 - 1876	William Hodson	1954 - 1958	Fredrick Arthur Bidwell
1877 - 1878	Walter Moore	1958 - 1960	William James Francis Baxter
1878 - 1878	Arthur Hall	1961 - 1975	Alec Ernest Spencer
1879 - 1879	Charles Henry Teakle	1975 - 1986	Richard Charnley Taylor
1880 - 1882	William Turner		

WHITE HART TAP

The White Hart Tap was situated in Newnham Street at what was number 10, by the entrance to the cattle market. Today the site is the delivery access to the Cloisters shopping area.

1871 - 1871	Thomas Cornish	1908 -	C Vail
1872 -	James Cresswell	1920 -	Thomas Lucas
1900 -	A Topping	1940 -	F L Goddard
1902 - 1903	G Butler		

WHITE LION

The White Lion during the 1960's

At number 31, St Mary's Street, on the corner with Silver Street, stood the White Lion Inn. It dates from the mid 17th century.

A Norfolk woolcomber, Nicholas Mallabar had come to Ely about the middle of the century and was appointed master of the Workhouse or Spinning House, and here for some years he employed the poor of the City in the spinning of yarn. His business evidently met with considerable success, and after a few years, he began to acquire property in the city. Soon he acquired the Red Lion in the High Street and some considerable property at the Bray's Lane corner of the Market Place; later he was chosen as High Sherriff of the County. In 1679 Nicholas Mallabar was occupying a tenement in Walpole Lane (Silver Street) next to the White Lion. In fact there is every reason to believe that he also owned the inn itself, for when in the year 1722 at a Court of the Manor of Ely Barton it was presented that the owner of this property, Robert Hindes, had died and his son Robert was admitted, the property was described as *"A Messuage or Tenement late Nicholas Mallabar"*. On the death of the younger Robert Hindes in 1767, the property passed to his son, Thomas:- *"A Messuage or Tenement called the White Lion in Ely St. Mary's, formerly Mallabar's"*.

It is interesting to speculate on the reason why the sign of The White Lion should have been adopted for the house. The property on the opposite corner of Silver Street, which had a frontage stretching from the corner of the street to the churchyard of St. Mary's had been from 1636 until 1660 in the possession of the Lord Protector Oliver Cromwell, whose family armorial bearings were in fact a white lion on a black shield. But perhaps it is mere coincidence that the owners of the adjacent property should have adopted the same heraldic device for their inn sign.

The Hindes supplied the White Lion with ale from their brewery on Waterside and when Elizabeth Olley took over the license she continued to supply her customers with ale from their brewery. During her tenancy, the White Lion was used regularly by bellringers and parishioners who gathered there to hold their vestry meetings. The White Lion remained in Hindes family possession, passing to James Hindes in 1774 with the exception of "*such part to which Thomas Olley was admitted on 12th October 1773*". This consisted of "*An Outhouse formally a Dovehouse, together with a piece of yard adjoining*". Thomas Olley appears to have purchased this part of the property, but he was in fact also occupying the inn as a tenant. A possible reason for his acquisition of this small part of the premises is provided when we recall at this period the new Turnpike roads were coming into their own. The road from Ely to Cambridge had been constructed only a few years before this date and whereas the main road had formerly turned into West End and passed along St. Johns Road to Witchford, it now took its present route straight up Cambridge Road to Stretham and so over the newly constructed bridge to Stretham ferry. The rise of the Lamb Inn, which from a small and rather insignificant house became the principal hotel in the city, was a direct result of the improved communications. As a posting-house for the long distance coaches from London to Lynn and Norwich the Lamb quickly rose to a prominent position in the city. The White Lion was too far from the centre of the town to compete for the coaching business, but it was ideally situated to command the traffic of the carriers carts and wagons which were then making increasing use of the new road. The new bridge which had supplanted Stretham ferry was not a very substantial construction of timber, and traffic over it was subjected to a weight restriction. There is little reason to doubt that Thomas Olley recognised the demands of the new conditions and supplied the needs of the users of the road by setting up some kind of weighing machine at the White Lion.

In 1836 a party was held at the White Lion to celebrate the introduction of gas street lighting to St.Mary's Parish.

The former White Lion Inn in 2006.

By 1875 it had become one of Henry Hall's many pubs and remained in the Hall family until 1930 when it merged in to the new firm of Hall, Cutlack & Harlock.

In the Return of Licensed Houses of 1906 it listed 2 bedrooms for the landlord's family and 4 for lodgers with stabling for 10 horses and 10 vehicles. The White Lion held a full alehouse license up to its closure by Watney Mann in March 1970. The property still stands and is currently in use as a Veterinary practise

1670 -	Nicholas Mallabar	1887 - 1888	William Turner
1722 -	Robert Hindes	1888 - 1895	William Peart
1767 -	Robert Hindes Jnr	1896 - 1898	Susan Jeffrey
1770 -	Thomas Olley	1899 - 1901	James Gillson
1773 - 1812	Elizabeth Olley	1903 - 1905	Fanny Fysh
1813 - 1822	John Olley	1906 - 1908	Rose B.E Pallant
1823 - 1847	Robert Griffin	1909 - 1919	Albert James Smith
184? - 1864	Elizabeth Griffin	1920 - 1924	Gertrude Maud Smith
1865 - 1883	William Howe	1925 - 1963	Leonard James Cross
1884 - 1884	John Coxall	1964 - 1965	Dennis John Jones
1885 - 1886	William Doe	1965 - 1970	Kenneth Corbett Craig

WHITE SWANN
Market Square

Not to be confused with the White Swan on Waterside, this Inn dates back to 17th century and once stood on the corner of Market Square and Brays Lane, where Woolworths is now. Very little reference to this Inn is to be found except that William Wagstaffe, who was a textile merchant and a churchwarden of Holy Trinity, died in 1675. Abigail his widow was in 1679 owning a tenement, which was called the White Swan. Abigail died on the 10th of April 1693, aged 78.

WHITE SWAN
Waterside

Number 47, Waterside used to be the White Swan. Early reference to the White Swan is from the Holy Trinity poor rates of 1786 and shows William Jeffrey paying rent £3.10s and a rate of 8/3.

The former White Swan Inn in 2007.

In 1844 the White Swan was "*To Be Let By Tender, and entered upon on the 29th September inst, the under mentioned desirable lots belonging to the governors of the Poor's Lands in Ely, and now in the occupation of Messrs Nash & Co of the town of Cambridge. Lot1. The Swan Inn and Public House situate near the Waterside, in the town of Ely, with the out houses, yard, stables, beer storehouse, blacksmiths shop and wharfage and crane belonging to the premises*".

In 1850 Coatman the carrier was advertising a service to Stretham on Thursdays from the Jolly Waterman.

The White Swan was again advertised to be let in 1852, as in the Cambridge Chronicle dated the 14th August that year, it was described as "*All that well-Accustomed, Old Licensed and Full Public House, known as the White Swan or Jolly Waterman situate near the Quay in the City of Ely with Stables, Blacksmiths shop, Landing-place, and convenient yard , and premises attached*'. Between 1846 and 1867 the pub was also known as the Jolly Waterman.

An entry in the Police licensing offences register in 1870 shows an entry for Reuben Vaughan, Victualler of Ely who "*having his house open for the sale of beer on 9th October at 11/40*', was fined 10/ with 11/6 costs.

Closed in 1871, today the former White Swan is a private residence.

1786 - 1798 William Jeffrey	1845 - 1845 Gregory Harrison
1799 - 1820 Mary Jeffrey	1848 - 1848 George Sherwin
1821 - 1821 John Dawson Ewer	1849 - 1855 Richard Lupson
1822 - 1823 George Thorpe	1856 - 1865 James Cooper
1824 - 1824 Robert Davy	1866 - 1866 William Thomas Lee
1825 - 1831 George Whitrow	1867 - 1867 Royal Lee
1832 - 1835 Thomas Fyson	1868 - 1868 Thomas Allen
1836 - 1843 Thomas Benton	1869 - 1869 William Willson
1844 - 1844 Charles Coates	1870 - 1871 Rueben Vaughan

WINDMILL

The Windmill public house was situated at number 48, Cambridge Road, opposite the Barton Road Junction. During the mid 19th century the area was known as Newtown. The pub took its name from the Windmill that stood opposite on Barton Road, formally known as Smock Mill Alley. Licensed as a beer house until closure, it was owned and supplied by Harlock's brewery until the mergers of the mid 1900's.

On 1st November 1842 Thomas Benstead was charged with "*offence against Beer Act*" and "*refusing to admit Pc Lees*" for which he was fined £2 and 11/6 costs and on 2nd September 1883, Joseph Henson was fined £3 and £3/15/6 costs for "*opening house before ½ past 12 on Sunday*".

The 1906 Returns of Licensed Houses listed it as having 3 bedrooms for the landlord and stabling for 1 horse. In the inter-war years, in common with many other pubs, the Windmill ran a Slate Club for its regulars.

The former Windmill public house in 2007.

When the East Anglian Breweries closed the Windmill on 31st August 1958, landlord Edward Moden moved to the George & Dragon. The property is today a private residence providing Bed and Breakfast for visitors to Ely.

1842 - 1847 Thomas Benstead
1850 - 1851 Thomas Roberts
1864 - 1870 John Hoggeard
1871 - 1892 Joseph Henson
1892 - 1896 William Davey
1896 - 1899 Fredrick William Quantrill
1900 - 1903 Mary Ann Sullivan

1904 - 1911 James White
1912 - 1928 Alfred Green
1929 - 1933 Lydia Green
1934 - 1938 Arthur J Rayner
1938 - 1956 George Edward Moden
1957 - 1958 Edward Moden

WOOLPACK

The Woolpack Inn circa 1960 and the building that now occupies the site in 2007.

On the corner of Market Street and Newnham Street where the Nat West Bank now stands, once stood the Woolpack Inn.

In 1747 mention is made of Thomas Chambers Inn keeper in a mortgage to Ann Benwell of Cambridge, widow, "*All that his messuage with appurtenances situate and lieing in Ely in a certain place called Newnham next a messauge next Austin Johnson, west. The south end abutting upon the street called High Row. The North part abbutts upon a messuage belonging to Browning. The east side thereof abutting on a street called Newnham*".

In 1852, the Woolpack Inn was one of the 10 Ely pubs auctioned off by Nash & Co of Royston. The sales catalogue shows it as Lot 26 and listed as *"A roomy Brick-and-Tile HOUSE and TWO TENEMENTS, in Newnham Street; together with a Shed, etc, at the end. The Inn Premises contain Two Front Parlours, Tap Room, Kitchen, Bar, Cellar, and Nine Bed Rooms; also the YARD and new-built Brick and Slate STABLING behind, with Lofts, affording accommodation for about Thirty Horses, with Lofts, two Pumps, etc. etc"*. Ebenezer W Harlock of Ely bought the Woolpack for 560 guineas.

Landlord Josiah Hippersley was in front of the magistrates on 12th February 1859 charged with assault upon Police Sergeant Hill, the case was discharged on payment of 7s costs. He was back in court again on 23rd September the same year, charged with 2 counts of *"having deficient measures"* and fined 12.6d with 12s 6d costs.

In 1906 the Woolpack was shown to have 3 bedrooms for the landlord's family and 5 bedrooms for lodgers with stabling for 12 horses and 6 vehicles.

The Woolpack held a full alehouse license and was supplied by Harlock's brewery until 1930, when the merger to Hall, Cutlack & Harlock took place. During his tenure, Walter Northrop was Secretary of the Ely and District License Victuallers Association and as landlord of the Woolpack he also ran a Thrift Club for his regulars.

In May 1969, under Watney Mann's rationalisation programme, the Woolpack closed its doors for the last time after more than 300 years of trading. The premises were demolished in 1971.

1747 - Thomas Chambers	1856 - 1857 James Curtis
1786 - William Parson	1858 - 1858 James Spooner
1790 - 1790 William Mendham	1859 - 1863 Josiah Hippersley
1791 - 1793 Thomas Mendham	1864 - 1875 William Pope
1794 - 1806 John Mendham	1876 - 1878 Eliza Pope
1807 - 1812 John Wingfield	1879 - 1880 Robert Atkin
1813 - 1814 Elizabeth Wingfield	1881 - 1884 George Galley
1815 - 1828 John Anderson	1885 - 1885 Ebenezer William Harlock
1829 - 1832 Robert Few	1886 - 1889 Robert White
1833 - 1835 Elizabeth Few	1890 - 1914 William Peacock
1836 - 1843 Edward Luddington	1915 - 1915 Rebecca Peacock
1844 - 1845 William Freeman	1916 - 1927 Percy Langford
1846 - 1847 Mrs Elizabeth Freeman	1927 - 1950 Walter Northrop
1848 - 1851 Thomas Hawkins	1950 - 1955 Henry Alfred Glover
1852 - 1852 William Dewey	1955 - 1968 George Peacock
1853 - 1855 Samuel Kingston	1968 - 1969 Alfred James Victory